Log Cabins
New Techniques for Traditional Quilts

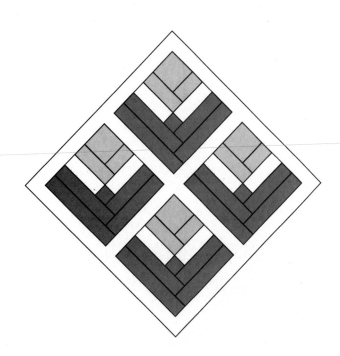

by Janet Kime

Cutting Edge Quilt Designs, Inc.

Credits

Photography	Mark Frey
Illustrations	Chuck Eng, Janet Kime
Hand model	Rochelle Munger

Photograph of the author by Ted Larson. Cover design by Chuck Eng.

Acknowledgments

Many thanks to those of my students, family, and friends who completed quilts for this book, sometimes under duress! Your suggestions and good humor were always appreciated.

Joel Patz, Virginia Morrison, and Ken Etzkorn read the manuscript and made valuable comments. Thanks also to Dick Newcomb, The Guru of Grammar.

My deepest gratitude to Marilyn Doheny, my first, best, and favorite quilting teacher, for her continuing encouragement and support.

Quilts not otherwise identified are by the author. The following people generously allowed the quilts they own to appear in this book: Barbara Felker, Don and Rachel Goldstein, Tom and Margaret Hodnett, Ric Hoffman, Donna Klemka and Martin Baker, Lindsay Michimoto, Sharon Redeker, and Connor Tee.

Front cover: **Vashon Interweave**, *page 107.*
Back cover: **Red Hot Stars**, *1991, 55" x 64". Directions on page 132.*

Log Cabins: New Techniques for Traditional Quilts©
©1992 by Janet Kime

Cutting Edge Quilt Designs, Inc.
P.O. Box 75
Edmonds, Washington 98020

Printed in the United States of America.

Kime, Janet
      Log Cabins / Janet Kime; [photography, Mark Frey; illustration and graphics, Chuck Eng, Janet Kime].
      p.   cm.
   ISBN 0-945169-11-6:
   1. Quilting—Patterns. 2. Patchwork—Patterns. I. Title.

Library of Congress Catalog Card Number 92-72474

Contents

Quilt Design and Fabric Selection   1

The Basic Log Cabin Block   15
Instructions: Basic Log Cabins   23

Rectangular Log Cabins   33
Instructions: Rectangular Log Cabins   37

Courthouse Steps   39
Instructions: Courthouse Steps   41

Off-Center Log Cabins   49
Instructions: Off-Center Log Cabins   53

Irregular Log Cabins   93
Instructions: Irregular Log Cabins   95

Chimneys and Cornerstones   97
Instructions: Chimneys and Cornerstones   101

Thick-and-Thin   111
Instructions: Thick-and-Thin   113

Cabin Stars   121
Instructions: Cabin Stars   131

Borders   141

Quilting Designs   145

Quiltmaking Techniques   149

for Mother

Introduction

Log Cabin is one of the most popular pieced quilt designs. Traditional log cabin blocks are easy to construct and have no unruly bias edges or triangle points to match, making a log cabin quilt a suitable project for the beginning quiltmaker; but the blocks can be arranged in a virtually infinite number of ways, allowing the advanced quiltmaker to experiment with principles of color and design. Log cabin quilts can be primitive or elegant, subdued or noisy, comfortingly simple or stunningly complex.

I have included in this book only log cabin quilts that start with a center square or rectangle, omitting those based on diamonds or triangles. I have likewise not included curved log cabins or pineapple log cabins. All of the log cabin quilts in this book, except Cabin Stars and the slapdash Irregular Log Cabin, are constructed of simple squares and rectangles.

There are no templates in this book; only rotary-cutting instructions are provided. Since nearly all of the pieces are squares and rectangles, for which I provide measurements, you could draw templates on graph paper if you do not have a rotary cutter. If you plan to make more than one small quilt, however, I hope you will purchase rotary equipment. In all the classes I have taught, I have yet to meet a quilter who tried rotary cutting and then went back to using templates. Rotary cutting is not just a gadgety way to cut your fabric; it is *much* faster and *much* more accurate. Almost all quilt shops offer introductory classes on rotary cutting. A log cabin quilt makes an excellent first project for a quiltmaker new to rotary cutting. You will be able to prepare your pieces so quickly, you will be unable to imagine why anyone would do it any other way.

In this book I present instructions for eight types of log cabin quilts: basic log cabin, rectangular log cabin, Courthouse Steps, off-center log cabin, irregular log cabin, Chimneys and Cornerstones, Thick-and-Thin, and Cabin Stars. In each section I describe the construction of the basic block, with many hints to help you along. Each variation is illustrated with several quilts, all with notes about their construction. With the information provided you should be able to make any of the quilts in this book, modify them, or use the basic instructions to create your own designs.

Even if you have already made one or more log cabin quilts, you should read through the introductory chapter on log cabin design; you'll find some good information about planning quilts and selecting fabric. Then read the chapter on basic log cabins. The construction technique I use in all of the variations is introduced there.

I hope you enjoy the variations and the quilts that illustrate them, and find yourself rooting through your fabric collection to try yet another version. There are so many possibilities, as I was planning this book I found it difficult to stop sewing and start writing!

Friends in the Forest *by Corki Duncan; color plate on page 62, instructions on page 27.*

Quilt Design and Fabric Selection

The traditional log cabin block starts with a small center square to which rectangles ("logs") are added, building the block in a spiral from the center out. Each rectangle is added to the next adjacent side, moving either clockwise or counterclockwise, until the desired size is achieved. The completed block is square.

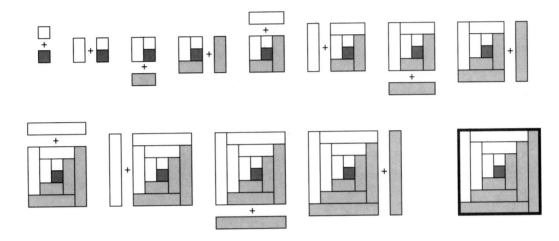

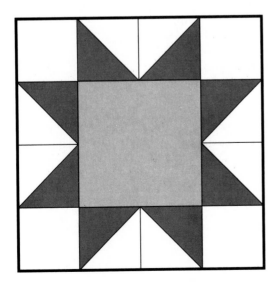

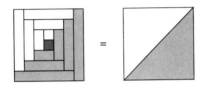

In the traditional block, the logs are added in the order two light, two dark, two light, and so on, resulting in a block divided diagonally into half light, half dark. Each block can be viewed as a square composed of two "half-square" triangles.

Half-square triangles are the basis of many traditional quilt patterns, and many log cabin quilts use these designs.

1

There are several overall patterns that are thought of as traditional log cabin designs. Some of these are illustrated on page 3. Notice that in each of these designs there is only one basic block; the different patterns are created simply by turning the blocks to the four positions shown here.

The number of possible arrangements of the blocks in even a 36-block log cabin quilt is enormous. To experiment with your own log cabin designs, cut some squares of cardboard or template plastic (2" square is a convenient size), color half of each with a felt-tip marker, and arrange them to your heart's content.

Center square

The center square of the log cabin block is often a contrasting color, adding another design element to the quilt. The centers can provide regularly spaced dots of color across the surface of the quilt, as you can see in the designs on page 3.

An interesting effect can be achieved by moving the "center" to a different position in the block. In Peter's Quilt (page 60), a Barn-Raising design, the red square that would normally be the center of each block is used instead as the first log. As the blocks are rotated, the position of the red square changes. In a design such as Barn Raising, where all four positions are used, the contrasting squares seem to dance over the surface of the quilt.

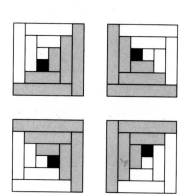

The center square of the log cabin block may be the same width as the logs, or larger. Large center squares can interrupt the lines of a traditional design in an interesting manner. Compare this design to the Barn Raising on the next page.

The quilt Toys (page 61) is an example of a basic log cabin with even larger center squares. When the centers are this large or larger, the logs appear to be the setting in which the "blocks" (actually the centers) are arranged. The result is a quilt quite different from a traditional log cabin.

Barn Raising

Light and Dark

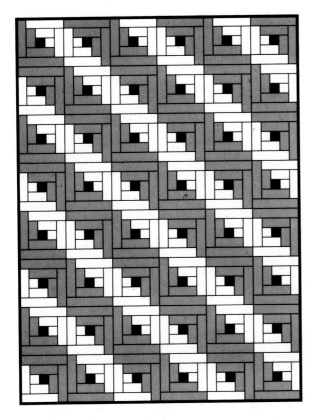

Straight Furrows

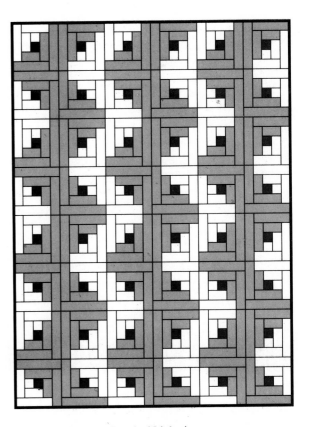

Streak o' Lightning

Log width

In the traditional block, all the logs are cut the same width. Blocks made of relatively few, wide logs have a more pronounced stairstep effect than blocks of the same size made of narrower logs.

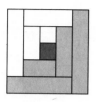 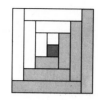

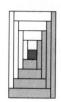 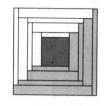

If you wish to experiment with individual block designs, try varying the width of the logs within the block as well as the centers.

Thick-and-Thin log cabins, which are covered in detail in a later chapter, are made of blocks in which either the dark or light logs are one-half the width of the other logs. This produces a curve dividing the two halves of the block, instead of a straight diagonal.

I construct most of my log cabin quilts using finished log widths of 1", 1 $\frac{1}{4}$", or 1 $\frac{1}{2}$". Narrower logs are attractive but more difficult to sew accurately. Logs as wide as 2" or 2 $\frac{1}{2}$" can look clunky, and as though the only consideration were finishing the quilt as quickly as possible. In general, I use narrower log widths for small pieces such as wall hangings, and wider logs for lap quilts and bed quilts.

Number of rounds

Block size is determined by the log width, the size of the center square, and the number of rounds. In the traditional block, block size is usually increased in rounds. Each round increases the size of the block by twice the finished log width.

 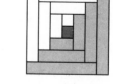 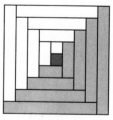

2 rounds   3 rounds   4 rounds

Although I have occasionally used log cabin blocks with only two rounds around the center, I think it takes at least three rounds to develop a clear overall design. Many log cabin quilts from the 1800's have a large number of rounds and logs only $\frac{1}{2}$" wide, greatly reducing the stairstep effect and producing clean and bold overall designs.

To modify the size of the block, you can also stop at half rounds. Notice that the starting square is not in the exact center of these blocks. Notice also that the last logs added determine which half of the block is larger. For a further discussion of this, see page 15.

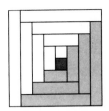

1 ½ rounds   2 ½ rounds   3 ½ rounds

If your design does not require a small center, small adjustments in block size can be made by altering the size of the center square.

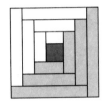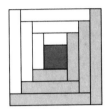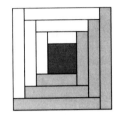

Quilt size

As you plan a log cabin quilt, four factors affect the final size of the quilt: the size of the center square, the width of the logs, the number of rounds in the block, and the number of blocks in the quilt.

I usually start with a general idea of how big I want the quilt to be: 40" wide or less (wall quilt or baby quilt), 50-60" wide (lap quilt), or 70-90" wide (bed quilt). I then select the overall design and the log width I would prefer. I often use 1" logs and have three rounds plus a small center, which makes a 7" block, so I start with 7" blocks in the initial plan. Often in this first plan the quilt is too big or too small, and I must decide what to change.

<table>
<tr><td>

To *decrease* the size of the quilt:

1. Decrease the size of the center square. (It cannot be less than the log width.)
2. Decrease the log width.
3. Decrease the number of rounds in each block, or remove one half of the last round. (Removing half a round will affect your design; see page 15.)
4. Eliminate entire rows of blocks from the design.

</td><td>

To *increase* the size of the quilt:

1. Increase the size of the center square. Redraw at least a section of your quilt, to be sure you like the effect.
2. Increase the log width.
3. Increase the number of rounds in each block.
4. Add rows of blocks to the design.

</td></tr>
</table>

If you decide to add or eliminate rows of blocks from your design, make a sketch to be sure you like the effect. Most of the traditional designs are symmetrical, and require an even number of rows both horizontally and vertically. If you eliminate only one row, your design may become asymmetrical. This *can* be a pleasing change, and can add a lot of interest to a wall hanging. See, for example, Pinks and Purples on page 82.

Yardage requirements

When it comes to calculating the yardage of each fabric needed for a quilt, many quilters are simultaneously bewildered and consumed by anxiety. Admittedly, nice fabrics are expensive and you don't want to purchase five yards too much. On the other hand, you must allow for cutting mistakes and you might want to have some left over to add to your fabric stash. My first quilting instructor calculated our yardages to a hair. I purchased a beautiful green print for my class project and had enough for the quilt, but only a $1/2$" sliver left over. I would have loved to use the fabric in other projects since and have searched high and low, but have never found more. I have never forgiven her!

Log cabin quilts can be roughly divided into three types:
1. Controlled designs, where the same fabric is used in the same position in each block.
2. Designs where either the light logs or the dark logs or both are all cut from one fabric.
3. Scrap quilts.

The first method on page 8 is used to calculate the yardages for controlled designs, where, for example, fabric D is used always and only for the last dark log. You must repeat the calculation for each fabric.

The second method on page 9 is used when half the block is cut from one fabric, or when you need an estimate of the total yardage necessary for a scrap quilt.

Many quilters are intimidated by math, but if you follow the directions step by step you will be fine. An inexpensive hand calculator makes the task much easier. *If you can triple a recipe, you can calculate yardages.*

If pages 8 and 9 simply give you the willies and you don't have a friend (or an offspring) who would enjoy figuring your yardages, you can use the estimates on the bottom of page 9 for your log cabin quilt. If you are *really* undecided about your quilt design, and just want a general idea of how much fabric you might need for a quilt, you can employ my quick-and-dirty method for calculating yardages. →

The Quick-and-Dirty Method of Yardage Calculation:

1. **Figure out how much yardage you must buy for the back of the quilt.**

2. **Multiply that by 3 for the front of the quilt.**

See page 151 for information about planning the back of your quilt. You need about three times more fabric for the front than you need for the back because of all the seams on the front; those seam allowances eat up a lot of fabric. Of course, the Quick and Dirty method provides only a wild estimate; for most quilts, it is a very generous estimate, and you will have some fabric left over. You might have a lot of fabric left over. If *that* gives you the willies, calculate your yardages.

Fabric selection

Fabric selection for log cabin quilts can be a lot of fun, because there are so many ways to play with the designs.

Scrappy vs. planned   One of the first decisions you must make with each quilt is whether you will use a narrow selection of fabrics, or a wide variety, or something in between.

There are many ways to define scrap quilts, but I think the most useful is this: *a scrap quilt is a quilt in which the same fabric does not appear in the same position in every block.* To make a scrappy log cabin quilt, you cut each size of log from several fabrics, then choose from the stack randomly as you assemble the blocks. If you are working with many fabrics, you will be able to avoid placing two logs of the same fabric next to each other. If you are working with only a half dozen darks (or lights), it takes more effort to ensure that two logs of the same fabric don't touch when you sew the blocks together. I generally don't worry about this too much. In the quilt Vashon Interweave (page 81) there are only five green fabrics, five fuchsias, and six teals, and there are many places where two logs of the same fabric touch.

If you have a large fabric collection, scrappy log cabins are fun. If you don't, you will find it easier to sew planned blocks, where several fabrics may be used but each block is identical. In a three-round log cabin block there are six light logs, six dark logs, and a center square. If you choose a different fabric for each log position, you will have almost as much visual texture in your quilt as you would if it were entirely scrappy. See the topmost block in the photograph and the quilt Pine Trees (page 75).

A different fabric for each log might be too much texture for your taste. The easiest way to tone the block down is to use one fabric for all of the light logs or all of the dark logs. See the next block down in the photograph.

The block is calmed down even further if you use the same fabric for each pair of logs; this is often called the chevron method. The final option in this progression, of course, is to use one fabric for all of the light logs and another fabric for all of the dark logs, as in the bottom block in the photograph.

Sophisticated Lady (page 64) is an example of a two-fabric log cabin. The printed fabric used for the dark, and the subtle printed muslin used for the light, introduce some visual texture. Two-fabric log cabins made from two solid fabrics are even more striking and can be very elegant.

If you use many fabrics in each log cabin block, the quilt will have a lot of visual texture. Tone down the quilt by using fewer fabrics in each block.

7

Determining Yardages for Log Cabin Quilts

Because log cabin quilts are made of simple rectangles, it is relatively easy to determine the yardage required for a quilt. The logs are cut from selvage-to-selvage strips that are all the same width, so you have only to figure out how many cuts you need.

My over-riding principle is that too much fabric is better than too little. Base all your calculations on 40"-wide fabric; it is not only safer, but also makes the calculations easier. After you make the calculation, increase the amount of fabric you need by at least 25%, to allow for miscuts and design changes. For example, if you determine that you need 1 yard, buy 1 1/4 yard. To add on 25%, use your hand calculator and multiply the yardage by 1.25. Or, divide the yardage calculated in half, then in half again, and add that amount.

Before you can accurately calculate your yardages, you must design your quilt. I know this is a great disappointment, but it is true. You must know the measurements of each log and the number of blocks in your quilt. If the fabric sale starts in five minutes and you know only that you want to make a log cabin quilt, you can use the estimates at the bottom of the next page. No one, however, will sympathize with you when you discover a month later that you need 2 yards more of the green stripe because it is the fabric you have decided you *must* use for the border, and the store has sold it all. At least rough out your design before you buy fabric. If you later decide to use 1" logs instead of 1 1/4", or make 72 blocks instead of 64, your extra yardage should carry you through.

For our sample quilt, we need 36 blocks. Cut width of the logs is 1 1/2", finished width 1". The centers are cut 1 1/2" x 1 1/2". The log measurements are listed at right.

Method #1

Use this method to calculate the yardage needed for each particular log in the block. This is the method to use if, for example, a particular dark print is used always and only for the last dark log.

1. Determine how many of the logs you can get from each selvage-to-selvage cut of fabric. For example, if the cut length of the log is 5 1/2", you can get 7 from each cut. Round all fractions down; you cannot use 0.27 of a log.

    $$\frac{40"}{\text{length of log}} = \text{\# logs/cut}$$

    $$\frac{40"}{5.5} = 7.27 = 7$$

2. Divide the total number of logs you need by the number of logs you can get from each cut. For example, if you need 36 logs (for 36 blocks) and can get 7 logs from each cut, you need 5.14 cuts. The fabric store is not going to sell 0.14 of a cut; you will have to make 6 cuts to get 36 logs. This time, round all fractions up.

    $$\frac{\text{total \# logs}}{\text{\# logs/cut}} = \text{\# cuts}$$

    $$\frac{36}{7} = 5.14 = 6$$

3. Multiply the number of cuts you need by the width of each cut. The cut width here is 1 1/2", so you need 9" of fabric.

    # cuts x cut width
    = inches of fabric

    $$6 \times 1.5" = 9"$$

Light logs

1 1/2" x 1 1/2"
1 1/2" x 2 1/2"
1 1/2" x 3 1/2"
1 1/2" x 4 1/2"

Dark logs

1 1/2" x 2 1/2"
1 1/2" x 3 1/2"
1 1/2" x 4 1/2"
1 1/2" x 5 1/2"

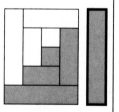

Now, 9" of fabric is 1/4 yard, but you have to wash and dry it, and clean up the edge before you rotary cut, and you may mismeasure and make one cut only 1" wide and have to throw it away. Adding 25% brings the yardage up to 11 1/4". Buy at least 1/3 yard (12").

Method #2

Use this method to calculate the yardage needed for a group of logs in the block. This is the method to use if, for example, all of the light logs are cut from the same fabric.

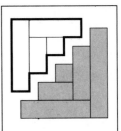

1. For one block, add up the lengths of the logs that will be cut from one fabric. In the sample block, the sum of the lengths of the light logs is 12".

total the log cut lengths

$1 \frac{1}{2}" + 2 \frac{1}{2}"$
$+ 3 \frac{1}{2}" + 4 \frac{1}{2}"$
$= 12"$

2. Multiply the length of the logs in one block by the number of blocks in the quilt. This gives you the total length of the logs in the whole quilt, as if they were laid together end to end. For our 36-block quilt, the total is 432".

total log length per block
x # blocks
= total log length

12" x 36 = 432"

3. Divide the total log length by 40" to get the number of cuts needed. In the sample, this is 10.8 cuts. You can't make 0.8 of a cut, so round all fractions up. You need 11 cuts.

$$\frac{\text{total log length}}{40"} = \text{# cuts}$$

$$\frac{432"}{40"} = 10.8 = 11$$

4. Multiply the number of cuts you need by the width of each cut. The cut width here is 1 ½", so you need 16 ½" of fabric.

 # cuts x cut width
= inches of fabric

11" x 1.5"/cut
= 16.5"

Adding 25% to 16 ½", the total is 21". Buy at least ²/₃ yard (24").

Method #2 is not as accurate as method #1 because it assumes that you can cut your logs from a continuous long strip of fabric, when in fact you must cut them from 40" lengths and there will be some waste. To minimize waste, cut the longest logs first and cut the shorter ones from the leftover ends of each cut.

Yardage Estimates

If you do not have time to plan your quilt before you must buy your fabric, the chart below lists the approximate yardages required for a log cabin quilt with 1" to 1 ½" finished logs and no border.

	light fabrics	dark fabrics
wall quilt (40" x 40")	1 ½ yards	2 yards
lap quilt (60" x 60")	3 yards	3 ½ yards
bed quilt (80" x 100")	5 yards	6 yards

Light/dark If you are striving for a traditional log cabin appearance, it is important that the light and dark halves of the blocks be distinct. You may use more than one color in each half, as well as a variety of prints, but as you collect fabrics you should have a light stack and a dark stack. For each fabric, there should be no doubt which stack it belongs in.

For example, in the selection of fabrics in the photograph the darks could be used for the dark half of log cabin blocks, and the muslin for the light half. The large flowered print would not be a good choice to include in either half. There is so much white background in it that it would not blend with the other darks, and the large, dark flowers would prevent it from blending with the light.

For most log cabin quilts you will want to select fabrics that clearly make a light group and a dark group. The large-scale print here does not fit with either the darks or the light, and if used in a log-cabin quilt would jump out from the design.

Now that I have provided you with this little rule, you can break it whenever you like. The quilt Bigger and Better (page 82) uses a contrasting fabric for one of the lights as well as the cornerstones. Use of a distinctive fabric that jumps out from the other lights or darks can produce a secondary pattern that adds a great deal of interest to the quilt, if the fabric is used in the same position in each block. The outer logs are often used to create a secondary design.

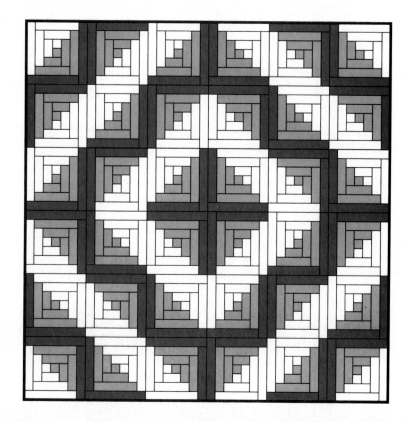

A fabric which stands out from the rest of the dark or light fabrics can be used to create an interesting secondary design. Here, the outermost dark logs are drawn in a darker shade.

10

Big City Blues (page 65) is an example of a quilt where the distinction between the light and dark halves of the blocks is fuzzy at best. Close up, it is difficult to see the Streak o' Lightning design of this quilt, and even at a distance the lines are blurred. This affect was achieved by lowering the contrast between the two halves of each block, using medium and medium-dark fabrics, for example, instead of lights and darks.

In general, however, you will want to make the two halves of your log cabin blocks distinct, so that your overall design doesn't get lost. The more complicated overall designs, and the ones with isolated dark or light triangles, are the easiest to lose in a low-contrast quilt.

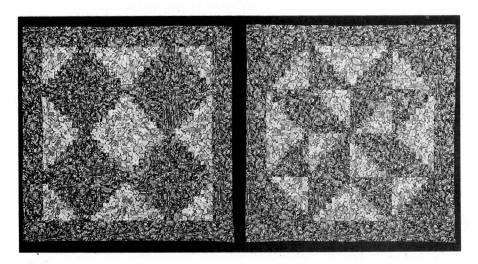

The design of the Light-and-Dark quilt on the left is relatively easy to see in spite of the low contrast between the fabrics, because the dark and light halves of the log cabin blocks are grouped together. The more complicated design on the right is more difficult to distinguish.

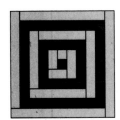 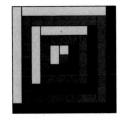

Light and dark values can also be used within each half of the log cabin block to produce secondary patterns. In many log cabin quilts from the 1800's the fabrics were carefully chosen to create strong concentric squares within the blocks. Spiral Courthouse Steps (page 40) is an example of a design created within the block by the arrangement of light and dark logs.

Print scale

Many wonderful medium- and large-scale print fabrics are now available to quilters. These prints, particularly ones with high contrast between the pattern and the background, can break up the outlines of a pieced block so that the stairstep effect of log cabin block almost disappears.

Large-scale prints can be used to break up the stairstep effect of the log cabin block.

When large-scale prints are cut into small pieces, one piece can look very different from another. These differences add a great deal of visual interest to your quilt, as certain portions of the print appear unpredictably here and there.

One of the blue fabrics in Toys (page 61) is a large-scale floral print. Splashes of big pink flowers appear in only some of the logs cut from the fabric, and tend to lead your eyes around surface of the quilt.

Logs cut from a large-scale print can vary widely, adding to the visual texture of your quilt.

Geometrics

Geometric prints, especially stripes, are fun to use in log cabin quilts. Many of the prints produced for quilters are floral designs with graceful curves. Straight-line designs such as stripes, checks, plaids, zig-zags, triangles, and other geometrics, provide interesting contrast. Stripes are particularly effective in log cabin quilts, where they can emphasize the shape of the long, narrow logs.

Because it is difficult to line up the designs when rotary cutting, most people avoid using geometrics in speed-pieced quilts. They are easy to use in log cabin quilts, however, if you cut the logs parallel to the selvages. To do this, make a wide cut from the yardage the desired *length* of the logs, then crosscut the individual logs so that the stripes run lengthwise down the logs.

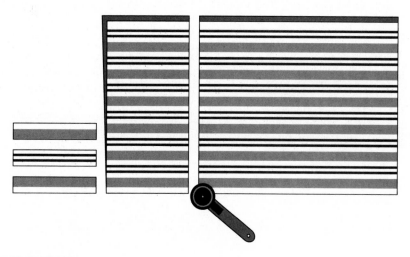

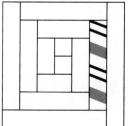

Cutting logs with the stripes lengthwise not only accents the log shape, but also makes it easier to keep the stripes aligned as you sew. If the stripes are cut crosswise, they tend to be pulled out of kilter as the next log is added.

Striped fabrics are very effective in log cabin quilts. When the stripes run lengthwise down the log, they can be used to create subtle and interesting secondary designs.

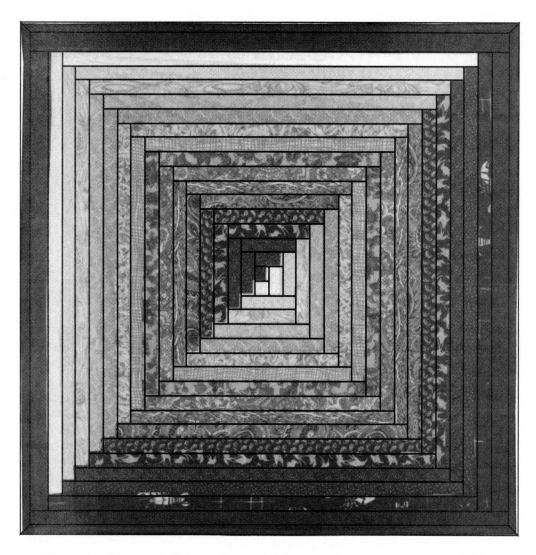

Say When; color plate on page 60, instructions on page 26.

The Basic Log Cabin Block

The basic log cabin block is constructed in a spiral, starting with a center square and adding rectangles ("logs") to successive adjacent sides. The logs are usually added in the order two light, two dark, two light, two dark, etc. The completed block is square.

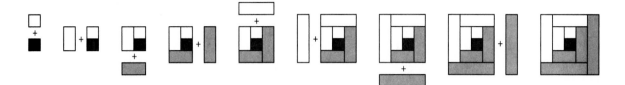

Four logs constitute a round. A log cabin block can consist of any number of rounds. Most log cabin quilts use three or four rounds, enough to establish the overall pattern of the quilt but not so many that assembling each block becomes tedious.

The block can be assembled either clockwise or counterclockwise. All the blocks for a given quilt should be assembled in the same manner unless the design dictates otherwise. Some of the designs in this book can be achieved only by piecing some of the blocks clockwise and some counterclockwise, and some designs are easier to cut and sew if the blocks are mixed. Most of the designs in this book are pieced in one direction, usually counterclockwise. If you make more than one log cabin quilt, it is best to select either clockwise or counterclockwise piecing and make all your quilts that way. After a while it becomes a habit, and one less thing you have to think about as you are sewing blocks together.

Note that one half of the block is larger than the other half. In each log cabin quilt you make, you must decide which half of the block you want to be dominant in the quilt: the light or the dark. In this book the dark half of the block is usually drawn as the larger half, because often the dark half of the quilt is the design fabric(s), and the light half can be thought of as background fabric(s).

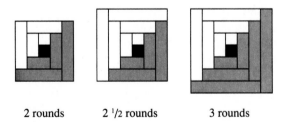

2 rounds   2 ½ rounds   3 rounds

If you start with the center square, then two light logs, then two dark logs, and proceed in that manner, you will end up with a block in which the dark half is larger. If you start the same way but stop in the middle of a round (2 ½ rounds, for example), the light half of the block will be larger. Notice that if you stop at a half round, the "center" is no longer in the exact center of the block.

To make the light half of the block larger using full rounds, start with the center square, two darks, two lights, etc. Notice that, unlike the 2 ½ round block above, the starting square is in the center, and is now positioned in the light half of the block.

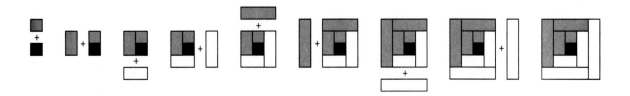

Construction Techniques

There are two ways to assemble log cabin blocks, which can be summarized as sew-then-cut (also called speed piecing), or cut-then-sew. Although I always cut-then-sew, I'll first describe the speed-piecing method.

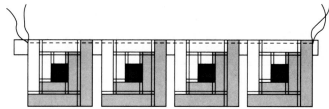

Sew-Then-Cut In this method, the logs are not cut individually. Instead, each log is added by sewing partial blocks to a long strip of fabric, right sides together. The strip is then cut, separating the blocks.

The main objection to this method is that it can be inaccurate, especially for inexperienced quilters. Unless you are a very accurate piecer, to keep the blocks from becoming too large or too small you must measure each one after each log is added, as you cut the blocks apart. This is so much trouble that most people just sew and whack, and the blocks end up too big or too small, or an assortment of sizes.

In spite of its being referred to as a speed-piecing technique, I don't find that this method saves much time. In particular, I don't like having to hop between the sewing machine, the ironing board, *and* rotary equipment. And it doesn't work for scrap quilts, where many different fabrics are used.

If you have tried this method and had good results, however, by all means use it.

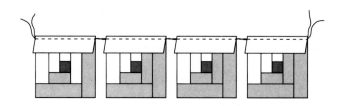

Cut-Then-Sew When I make a log cabin quilt, I precut all of the logs. I then chain-sew the same-size logs to all the blocks before proceeding to the next log.

If you rotary cut all the logs carefully, you know they are all the correct size. As you assemble the blocks, you may notice that the next log seems to be too short or too long. Actually, it isn't; it is the block that is too large or too small.

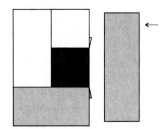

← If the log seems to be too short, you need to take a slightly wider seam allowance, maybe just a thread or two. Your block is too large, and taking wider seam allowances will make it smaller.

If the log seems to be too long, you need to take a slightly narrower seam allowance. Your block is too small, and taking narrower seam allowances will make it larger. →

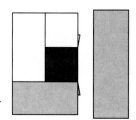

When you notice a problem developing, start to correct it immediately with the next log. As long as you can take seams at least $1/8$" wide, you probably do not need to rip out seams and start over.

As you add logs, keep using them to bring your block back to the correct size, adjusting the seam allowance until the logs match the developing block. If your last log fits perfectly, the block is the size you intended. After one block, you should have established the proper seam width, and there will be few problems with the other blocks.

Sample blocks The most dangerous hazard of the cut-then-sew method is the temptation to cut all of the logs before you sew a sample block. After all, much of time it takes to cut out the logs for a quilt is spent folding and unfolding fabric and evening up the edges, especially if you are using many fabrics in a scrap quilt. Once you are on a roll, so to speak, you will want to rotary cut everything. Don't do it!!

Yes indeed, I once cut all the logs for a quilt without sewing a sample block and they were all wrong. Even worse, I once gave a wrong measurement to a group of students, and everyone had to recut. Please, please sew a sample block. Even if you are positive the measurements are correct (and those particular students will never be again!), you will want to be sure you like the arrangement of the colors and fabrics. If a fabric in the sample block jumps out disturbingly from the rest, perhaps you can use it for a smaller log, or nestle it among the fabrics it is most similar to. You might see a linearity in a print you didn't notice before, and will know to cut all the logs in a certain direction. You might see that two fabrics are so similar they should not be side-by-side. You might see that there is not enough distinction between the dark and light halves of your block. This is the time to discover any problems and resolve them, not after you have cut all the logs for 72 blocks.

The sample block is also your opportunity to fine-tune your seam width. You can then breeze through the rest of the blocks.

> **Always sew a sample block before cutting all of the logs. This is The Voice of Experience speaking.**

> **Always add the next log to the side of the block that has two seams.**

Who's on first? You can refer to your sample block as you assemble the rest of the blocks. All sorts of mistakes can happen as you wend your way from the center to the last outer log, and students in my classes have made some very odd looking blocks indeed. There is a wonderful rule, however, that will help keep things progressing as they should: *always add the next log to the side of the block that has two seams.*

For the first few logs, you will need to carefully compare your block to your drawing, to be sure each log is added to the correct side. Starting with the last log of the first round, however, one and only one side of the block will have two seams. This is the side to which the next log is added.

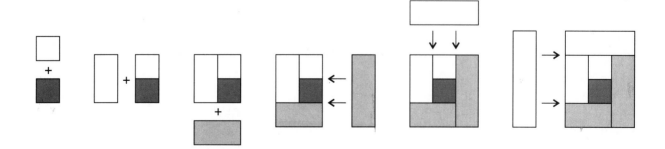

You still have to grab the correct log, but once you have it you will always know where to put it. In fact, it shouldn't be hard to locate the correct log, as the side with two seams will be on either the dark or light half of the block, and each log in each half is a different length. If you pay attention, only one log will fit.

Pressing The most important factor in assembling a good log cabin block, after you have figured out the proper seam allowance, is pressing as you go. ***Press after each log is added, before you add the next log.*** This is extremely important. In all machine piecing it is important to press each seam before it is crossed by another seam. In a log cabin block, the seam made as you add the next log always crosses the previous seam, so you must press after each log. It is tempting to just do a little finger-pressing and then add the next log. If you do this, there will be a little tuck at each seam intersection instead of a nice flat seam, and your block will be too small. There are some quilters who like the softer look of unpressed seams, and if you are among them you will have to take narrow seam allowances to end up with blocks the proper size.

> **Press after each log is added, before you add the next log.**

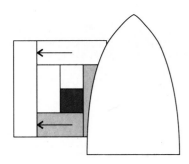

I myself belong to the flatten-it-to-death school of pressing. I usually press from the back first and then finish on the front, pushing the iron sideways into the bump of the seam allowance and flattening it out. I use a hot iron on cottons and lots of steam.

Pressing after each seam is really only a bother with the sample log cabin block, when you must hop up and press after each seam. You will chain-piece the rest of the blocks in multiples of 10 or 30 or whatever, and can press 10 or 30 seams and then return to the machine and add the next logs. Think of it as good exercise, and a way to keep your feet from falling asleep.

The second rule of pressing log cabin blocks is ***always press the seam allowances toward the log just added***. For example, when you sew the first log to the center square, press the seam allowances toward the first log. When you add the second log, press the seam allowances toward the second log. And so on. Don't press toward the darker fabric, or the more lightweight fabric, or whatever else seems reasonable at the time. Always press toward the outside of the block.

> **Always press seam allowances toward the log just added.**

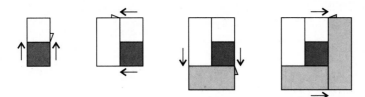

As you proceed, you will see that pressing the seam allowances toward the outside of the block is always pressing in the direction of least resistance. If you press toward the inside of the block, you will have some seam allowances doubled back on themselves, creating a lot of bulk you'd be better off without.

Strip-piecing the centers If you are using the same fabric for the centers and the first log throughout the quilt, you can strip piece the centers. Sew a strip of the center fabric to a strip of the fabric you are using for the first log, and press the seam allowances toward the log fabric. Press carefully, flattening out any bump from the right side. Then crosscut.

This avoids cutting out many little squares, sewing them together in pairs, and burning your fingers as you try to press each seam. The units will also be more accurate if they are strip-pieced, because you press before you cut. Small units are easily distorted at the ironing board.

If you are using a variety of fabrics for the centers and/or the first logs, you may still want to strip-piece shorter lengths and make 6 or 10 or 20 units from each combination. In a quilt with many blocks, the center combinations do not all have to be different.

The width of the log strip and the width of the crosscuts are both the *cut* width of the logs, which we will now discuss.

Log Measurements

To determine the measurements of the logs, draw your block full-size on $\frac{1}{4}$" gridded graph paper. If necessary, tape two or more sheets together, carefully matching the grid lines, to make a large enough sheet. Draw the logs in their *finished* sizes, not including seam allowance. Shade in the dark and light logs. Label the center square "C", and number the logs: start with the first log, and number the logs in the order they will be added to the block.

With a ruler, measure each log and record the measurements. These are the finished measurements, and do not include seam allowance.

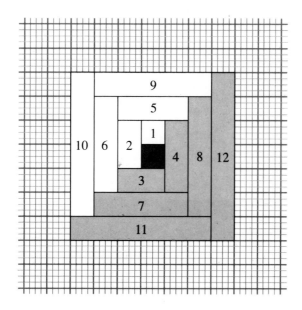

log #	light logs	dark logs
center		1" x 1"
1	1" x 1"	
2	1" x 2"	
3		1" x 2"
4		1" x 3"
5	1" x 3"	
6	1" x 4"	
7		1" x 4"
8		1" x 5"
9	1" x 5"	
10	1" x 6"	
11		1" x 6"
12		1" x 7"

Notice the patterns. There are two light logs, then two dark, then two light, etc. Each light log is a different length, and each dark log is a different length, but notice that there are two 2" logs, one light and one dark, and so on. Not counting the center, there is only one shortest log (1" light) and only one longest log (7" dark).

19

To determine the cut measurements of each log, including $1/4$" seam allowances, add $1/2$" to each dimension. For the block shown in the illustration on the last page, these are the finished and cut measurements of the logs.

LIGHT LOGS

log #	finished measurements	cut measurements
1	1" x 1"	1 1/2" x 1 1/2"
2	1" x 2"	1 1/2" x 2 1/2"
5	1" x 3"	1 1/2" x 3 1/2"
6	1" x 4"	1 1/2" x 4 1/2"
9	1" x 5"	1 1/2" x 5 1/2"
10	1" x 6"	1 1/2" x 6 1/2"

DARK LOGS

log #	finished measurements	cut measurements
3	1" x 2"	1 1/2" x 2 1/2"
4	1" x 3"	1 1/2" x 3 1/2"
7	1" x 4"	1 1/2" x 4 1/2"
8	1" x 5"	1 1/2" x 5 1/2"
11	1" x 6"	1 1/2" x 6 1/2"
12	1" x 7"	1 1/2" x 7 1/2"

Notice that within each color group in the example, each log is 1" longer than the previous log: *each log is a finished log width longer than the previous log*. This holds true for both finished measurements and cut measurements, and allows you to determine easily the measurements of additional logs, if you wish to add more rounds.

I recommend that you work your way through the block you use in your next log cabin quilt, calculating all the measurements. When you are done, you will have a very complete understanding of how the block is assembled, and you will be much less likely to be confused as you actually sew the pieces together.

Standard Block Measurements

For reference, the charts on the next page provide the finished and cut measurements for the dark and light logs of the block shown below, in the most common log widths. If you want to make a block with a larger center, draw it out and determine the cut measurement of each log. It isn't difficult.

Some common **finished widths** and **cut widths** of logs:

finished width	cut width
3/4"	1 1/4"
1"	1 1/2"
1 1/4"	1 3/4"
1 1/2"	2"
1 3/4"	2 1/4"
2"	2 1/2"

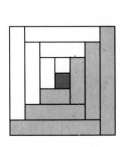

3-round block

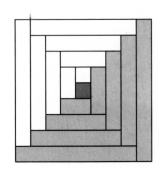

4-round block

Finished log width 1"
Cut log width   1 $^1/_2$"
3-round block   7" finished
4-round block   9" finished

	finished measurements	*cut measurements*
center	1" x 1"	1 $^1/_2$" x 1 $^1/_2$"
light logs	1" x 1"	1 $^1/_2$" x 1 $^1/_2$"
	1" x 2"	1 $^1/_2$" x 2 $^1/_2$"
	1" x 3"	1 $^1/_2$" x 3 $^1/_2$"
	1" x 4"	1 $^1/_2$" x 4 $^1/_2$"
	1" x 5"	1 $^1/_2$" x 5 $^1/_2$"
	1" x 6"	1 $^1/_2$" x 6 $^1/_2$"
	1" x 7"	1 $^1/_2$" x 7 $^1/_2$"
	1" x 8"	1 $^1/_2$" x 8 $^1/_2$"
dark logs	1" x 2"	1 $^1/_2$" x 2 $^1/_2$"
	1" x 3"	1 $^1/_2$" x 3 $^1/_2$"
	1" x 4"	1 $^1/_2$" x 4 $^1/_2$"
	1" x 5"	1 $^1/_2$" x 5 $^1/_2$"
	1" x 6"	1 $^1/_2$" x 6 $^1/_2$"
	1" x 7"	1 $^1/_2$" x 7 $^1/_2$"
	1" x 8"	1 $^1/_2$" x 8 $^1/_2$"
	1" x 9"	1 $^1/_2$" x 9 $^1/_2$"

Finished log width 1 $^1/_4$"
Cut log width   1 $^3/_4$"
3-round block   8 $^3/_4$" finished
4-round block   11 $^1/_4$" finished

	finished measurements	*cut measurements*
center	1 $^1/_4$" x 1 $^1/_4$"	1 $^3/_4$" x 1 $^3/_4$"
light logs	1 $^1/_4$" x 1 $^1/_4$"	1 $^3/_4$" x 1 $^3/_4$"
	1 $^1/_4$" x 2 $^1/_2$"	1 $^3/_4$" x 3"
	1 $^1/_4$" x 3 $^3/_4$"	1 $^3/_4$" x 4 $^1/_4$"
	1 $^1/_4$" x 5"	1 $^3/_4$" x 5 $^1/_2$"
	1 $^1/_4$" x 6 $^1/_4$"	1 $^3/_4$" x 6 $^3/_4$"
	1 $^1/_4$" x 7 $^1/_2$"	1 $^3/_4$" x 8"
	1 $^1/_4$" x 8 $^3/_4$"	1 $^3/_4$" x 9 $^1/_4$"
	1 $^1/_4$" x 10"	1 $^3/_4$" x 10 $^1/_2$"
dark logs	1 $^1/_4$" x 2 $^1/_2$"	1 $^3/_4$" x 3"
	1 $^1/_4$" x 3 $^3/_4$"	1 $^3/_4$" x 4 $^1/_4$"
	1 $^1/_4$" x 5"	1 $^3/_4$" x 5 $^1/_2$"
	1 $^1/_4$" x 6 $^1/_4$"	1 $^3/_4$" x 6 $^3/_4$"
	1 $^1/_4$" x 7 $^1/_2$"	1 $^3/_4$" x 8"
	1 $^1/_4$" x 8 $^3/_4$"	1 $^3/_4$" x 9 $^1/_4$"
	1 $^1/_4$" x 10"	1 $^3/_4$" x 10 $^1/_2$"
	1 $^1/_4$" x 11 $^1/_4$"	1 $^3/_4$" x 11 $^3/_4$"

Finished log width 1 $^1/_2$"
Cut log width   2"
3-round block   10 $^1/_2$" finished
4-round block   13 $^1/_2$" finished

	finished measurements	*cut measurements*
center	1 $^1/_2$" x 1 $^1/_2$"	2" x 2"
light logs	1 $^1/_2$" x 1 $^1/_2$"	2" x 2"
	1 $^1/_2$" x 3"	2" x 3 $^1/_2$"
	1 $^1/_2$" x 4 $^1/_2$"	2" x 5"
	1 $^1/_2$" x 6"	2" x 6 $^1/_2$"
	1 $^1/_2$" x 7 $^1/_2$"	2" x 8"
	1 $^1/_2$" x 9"	2" x 9 $^1/_2$"
	1 $^1/_2$" x 10 $^1/_2$"	2" x 11"
	1 $^1/_2$" x 12"	2" x 12 $^1/_2$"
dark logs	1 $^1/_2$" x 3"	2" x 3 $^1/_2$"
	1 $^1/_2$" x 4 $^1/_2$"	2" x 5"
	1 $^1/_2$" x 6"	2" x 6 $^1/_2$"
	1 $^1/_2$" x 7 $^1/_2$"	2" x 8"
	1 $^1/_2$" x 9"	2" x 9 $^1/_2$"
	1 $^1/_2$" x 10 $^1/_2$"	2" x 11"
	1 $^1/_2$" x 12"	2" x 12 $^1/_2$"
	1 $^1/_2$" x 13 $^1/_2$"	2" x 14"

Finished log width 2"
Cut log width   2 $^1/_2$"
3-round block   14" finished
4-round block   18" finished

	finished measurements	*cut measurements*
centers	2" x 2"	2 $^1/_2$" x 2 $^1/_2$"
light logs	2" x 2"	2 $^1/_2$" x 2 $^1/_2$"
	2" x 4"	2 $^1/_2$" x 4 $^1/_2$"
	2" x 6"	2 $^1/_2$" x 6 $^1/_2$"
	2" x 8"	2 $^1/_2$" x 8 $^1/_2$"
	2" x 10"	2 $^1/_2$" x 10 $^1/_2$"
	2" x 12"	2 $^1/_2$" x 12 $^1/_2$"
	2" x 14"	2 $^1/_2$" x 14 $^1/_2$"
	2" x 16"	2 $^1/_2$" x 16 $^1/_2$"
dark logs	2" x 4"	2 $^1/_2$" x 4 $^1/_2$"
	2" x 6"	2 $^1/_2$" x 6 $^1/_2$"
	2" x 8"	2 $^1/_2$" x 8 $^1/_2$"
	2" x 10"	2 $^1/_2$" x 10 $^1/_2$"
	2" x 12"	2 $^1/_2$" x 12 $^1/_2$"
	2" x 14"	2 $^1/_2$" x 14 $^1/_2$"
	2" x 16"	2 $^1/_2$" x 16 $^1/_2$"
	2" x 18"	2 $^1/_2$" x 18 $^1/_2$"

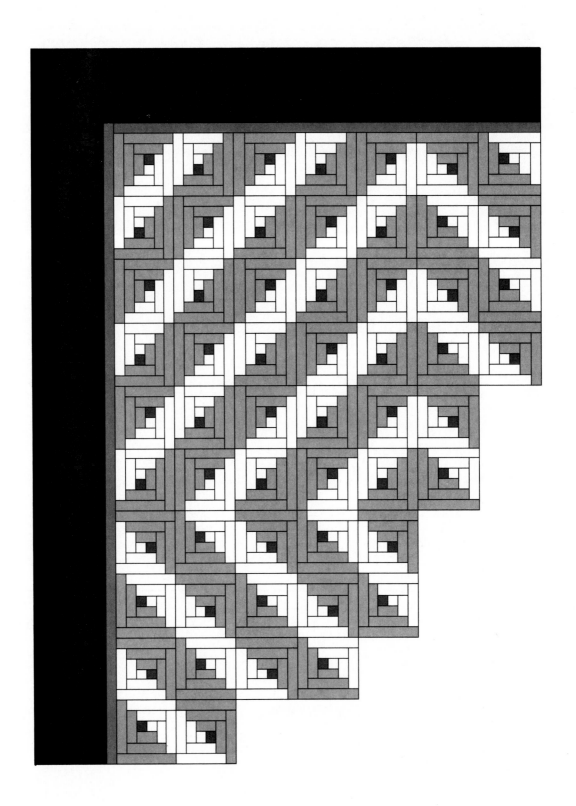

Peter's Quilt (page 60, instructions opposite).

Instructions: Basic Log Cabins

Peter's Quilt (page 60; diagram opposite)

I was intrigued by the placement of the red squares in this quilt. Instead of being the centers, the red squares are in the first log position. As the blocks are rotated to make the Barn-Raising design, the red squares seem to be sprinkled randomly over the surface of the quilt.

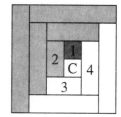

Quilt size	92" x 107"
Number of blocks	120
Block size	7 ¹/₂" finished
Log width	1 ¹/₄" finished
Number of rounds	2 ¹/₂,
Border	1 ¹/₄" inner border,
	7" outer border

Fabric required
- 4 yards total light fabrics
- 5 yards total dark fabrics
- ¹/₂ yard red fabric
- ²/₃ yard inner border fabric
- 2 yards outer border fabric
- 8 ¹/₂ yards backing fabric
- ³/₄ yard binding fabric

Cutting instructions

Cut 120 sets of logs from a variety of fabrics, following the measurements for 1 ¹/₄" finished logs on page 21 through the 6 ³/₄" light logs and the 8" dark logs. Use light fabrics for the centers. If you wish to strip piece the center/first log units you will need 6 strip units, each made of a selvage-to-selvage 1 ³/₄" cut of red and a similar cut of light fabric (see page 19).

Inner border: Piece 2 strips 1 ³/₄" x 76" and 2 strips 1 ³/₄" x 93".
Outer border: Piece 2 strips 7 ¹/₂" x 78 ¹/₂" and 2 strips 7 ¹/₂" x 107".

Toys (page 61)

A particularly pretty motif print was cut up for the centers of the log cabin blocks. The motifs determined the size of the center squares (5" finished in this quilt)) and the colors of the logs. If your motif print is a different size, draft your block and determine your log measurements.

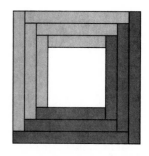

I used a different print for each log. For example, one particular print was used always and only for the first blue log. Using this many fabrics provides a scrappy look, but it takes much less time to cut the logs if you have to cut only one size from each fabric. Be sure you like the placement of the fabrics in the block before you cut.

A note of caution: if you use a motif fabric with a definite up-and-down for the centers, you cannot make identical blocks and simply rotate them into position. You must determine before you start how many blocks you need in each of the four positions. Look at the top row of blocks in the color photograph: from left to right, the blue is at bottom right, top left, top right, and bottom left. In this Barn-Raising quilt, there are four blocks in each of the four positions.

Quilt size	44" x 44"
Number of blocks	16
Block size	11" finished
Log width	1" finished, 5" centers
Number of rounds	3

Fabric required
- approximately 1 yard motif fabric
- ¹/₈-¹/₄ yard each of 6 light prints
- ¹/₈-¹/₃ yard each of 6 dark prints
- 1 ¹/₂ yards backing fabric
- ¹/₂ yard binding fabric

Cutting instructions

Light logs: Cut 16 sets.

1 ¹/₂" x 5 ¹/₂"	1 ¹/₂" x 8 ¹/₂"
1 ¹/₂" x 6 ¹/₂"	1 ¹/₂" x 9 ¹/₂"
1 ¹/₂" x 7 ¹/₂"	1 ¹/₂" x 10 ¹/₂"

Dark logs: Cut 16 sets.

1 ¹/₂" x 6 ¹/₂"	1 ¹/₂" x 9 ¹/₂"
1 ¹/₂" x 7 ¹/₂"	1 ¹/₂" x 10 ¹/₂"
1 ¹/₂" x 8 ¹/₂"	1 ¹/₂" x 11 ¹/₂"

Sophisticated Lady (page 64)

This elegant quilt is made from just two fabrics, a black-background print and a subtle white-on-muslin.

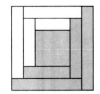

Quilt size	46" x 46"
Number of blocks	36
Block size	7" finished
Log width	1" finished; 3" centers
Number of rounds	2
Border	2"

Fabric required
 2 yards dark print (includes border and binding)
 1 yard light print
 2 yards backing fabric
 $1/2$ yard binding fabric

Cutting instructions
Centers: Speed piece the centers. You will need three strip units each made of a 3 $1/2$" cut of dark and a 1 $1/2$" cut of light. Crosscut every 3 $1/2$". (If your fabrics are more than 42" wide, you can make 12 crosscuts from each strip unit. If you can make only 11 crosscuts, you will need to piece three more center + light log units.)

Light logs: Cut 36 sets. The measurements start with the second light log.
 1 $1/2$" x 4 $1/2$"
 1 $1/2$" x 5 $1/2$"
 1 $1/2$" x 6 $1/2$"

Dark logs: Cut 36 sets.
 1 $1/2$" x 4 $1/2$"
 1 $1/2$" x 5 $1/2$"
 1 $1/2$" x 6 $1/2$"
 1 $1/2$" x 7 $1/2$"

Border: Cut 2 strips 2 $1/2$" x 42 $1/2$" and piece 2 strips 2 $1/2$" x 46 $1/2$".

Sawtooth Star (page 61)

This quilt includes log cabin blocks of different color combinations: there are eight navy/white blocks, four red/red, and four white/white. Although unpieced squares could be used where a 7" square of one color is needed, pieced log cabin blocks seem more appropriate and add visual texture. It doesn't really matter how the one-color blocks are oriented if they are constructed from one fabric, like the white blocks. The red blocks are arranged like the center of a Barn Raising, making an interesting cross in the center of the quilt (page 13).

Quilt size	42" x 42"
Number of blocks	16
Block size	7" finished
Log width	1" finished
Number of rounds	3
Border	1" inner border, 2" second border, 4" outer border

Fabric required
 $1/8$-$1/4$ yard each of 4 navy prints
 $1/8$-$1/4$ yard each of 7 red prints
 $1/2$ yard white
 1 $1/2$ yards border fabric (includes binding)
 1 $1/2$ yards backing fabric

Cutting instructions
Follow the measurements for 1" finished logs on page 21, through the 6 $1/2$" light logs and the 7 $1/2$" dark logs. Each log measurement is cut from a different fabric; so that all the blocks of a given color combination are identical.

Light logs: Cut 4 sets from red prints.
 Cut 12 sets from white.

Dark logs: Cut 8 sets from navy prints.
 Cut 4 sets from red prints.
 Cut 4 sets from white.

Borders: From white cut 2 strips 1 $1/2$" x 28 $1/2$" and 2 strips 1 $1/2$" x 30 $1/2$".
 From red cut 2 strips 2 $1/2$" x 30 $1/2$" and 2 strips 2 $1/2$" x 34 $1/2$".
 From the navy border print cut 2 strips 4 $1/2$" x 34 $1/2$" and 2 strips 4 $1/2$" x 42 $1/2$".

Old Fashioned Roses (page 64)

This is a simple Straight-Furrows design made of two different log cabin blocks. All of the blocks use the black-background rose print as the dark; half use scrappy pinks as the light, and the other half use scrappy greys.

		Fabric required
Quilt size	42" x 49"	2 ½ yards dark print (includes border and binding)
Number of blocks	20	
Block size	7" finished	½ yard total or scraps of pink prints
Log width	1" finished	½ yard total or scraps of grey prints
Number of rounds	3	1 ½ yards backing fabric
Border	1" inner border, 6" outer border	

Cutting instructions

Follow the measurements on page 21 through the 6 ½" light logs and the 7 ½" dark logs.
Light logs: Cut 10 sets from pink prints.
Cut 10 sets from grey prints.
Dark logs: Cut 20 sets from dark print.

Inner border: Cut 2 strips 1 ½" x 35 ½" and 2 strips 1 ½" x 30 ½".
Outer border: Cut 2 strips 6 ½" x 37 ½" and 2 strips 6 ½" x 42 ½".

Rainbow Lightning (page 59)

Large white centers dot the surface of this striking scrap quilt. Black prints used for the dark half of each block intensify the other colors. There are 16 blocks in each of five different colors.

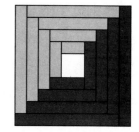

		Fabric required
Quilt size	76" x 96"	5 yards total black prints
Number of blocks	80	1 yard total prints in each of 5 colors: blue, yellow, red, pink, purple (includes binding)
Block size	10" finished	
Log width	1" finished, 2" centers	
Number of rounds	4	½ yard white
		6 yards backing fabric

Cutting instructions

Centers: Cut 80 squares 2 ½" x 2 ½".
Light logs: Cut 16 sets from assorted prints of each color; 5 colors x 16 sets each = 80 sets.

    1 ½" x 2 ½"
    1 ½" x 3 ½"
    1 ½" x 4 ½"
    1 ½" x 5 ½"
    1 ½" x 6 ½"
    1 ½" x 7 ½"
    1 ½" x 8 ½"
    1 ½" x 9 ½"

Dark logs: Cut 80 sets from assorted black prints.

    1 ½" x 3 ½"
    1 ½" x 4 ½"
    1 ½" x 5 ½"
    1 ½" x 6 ½"
    1 ½" x 7 ½"
    1 ½" x 8 ½"
    1 ½" x 9 ½"
    1 ½" x 10 ½"

Binding: Strip-piece scraps of different colors, then cut bias strips and join them end to end.

Say When (page 60)

This wallhanging is one big log cabin block. Although it looks like you just add rounds until you decide to stop you actually must plan ahead, because the order of the fabrics in the light half of the block is the exact reverse of the dark half.

Select 16 fabrics, choosing fabrics that can be arranged in a shaded progression from dark to light. Cut four logs from each fabric, two for the light half of the block and two for the dark half. From the darkest fabric cut only three logs, the two outer dark logs and the center square.

Quilt size	36" x 36"	**Fabric required**
Number of blocks	1	$^1/_8$-$^1/_4$ yard of each of 16 fabrics
Block size	32" finished	$^1/_3$ yard border fabric
Log width	1" finished	1 $^1/_4$ yards backing fabric
Number of rounds	16	$^1/_2$ yard binding fabric
Border	2"	

Cutting instructions
Label the 16 fabrics A through P, with A the darkest fabric. As you cut the logs, make separate stacks for side #1 and side #2. Stack #1 will be longest to shortest, and stack #2 will be shortest to longest.

	side 1	side 2
fabric A	1 $^1/_2$" x 32 $^1/_2$" 1 $^1/_2$" x 31 $^1/_2$"	1 $^1/_2$" x 1 $^1/_2$"
fabric B	1 $^1/_2$" x 30 $^1/_2$" 1 $^1/_2$" x 29 $^1/_2$"	1 $^1/_2$" x 2 $^1/_2$" 1 $^1/_2$" x 3 $^1/_2$"
fabric C	1 $^1/_2$" x 28 $^1/_2$" 1 $^1/_2$" x 27 $^1/_2$"	1 $^1/_2$" x 4 $^1/_2$" 1 $^1/_2$" x 5 $^1/_2$"
fabric D	1 $^1/_2$" x 26 $^1/_2$" 1 $^1/_2$" x 25 $^1/_2$"	1 $^1/_2$" x 6 $^1/_2$" 1 $^1/_2$" x 7 $^1/_2$"
fabric E	1 $^1/_2$" x 24 $^1/_2$" 1 $^1/_2$" x 23 $^1/_2$"	1 $^1/_2$" x 8 $^1/_2$" 1 $^1/_2$" x 9 $^1/_2$"
fabric F	1 $^1/_2$" x 22 $^1/_2$" 1 $^1/_2$" x 21 $^1/_2$"	1 $^1/_2$" x 10 $^1/_2$" 1 $^1/_2$" x 11 $^1/_2$"
fabric G	1 $^1/_2$" x 20 $^1/_2$" 1 $^1/_2$" x 19 $^1/_2$"	1 $^1/_2$" x 12 $^1/_2$" 1 $^1/_2$" x 13 $^1/_2$"
fabric H	1 $^1/_2$" x 18 $^1/_2$" 1 $^1/_2$" x 17 $^1/_2$"	1 $^1/_2$" x 14 $^1/_2$" 1 $^1/_2$" x 15 $^1/_2$"
fabric I	1 $^1/_2$" x 16 $^1/_2$" 1 $^1/_2$" x 15 $^1/_2$"	1 $^1/_2$" x 16 $^1/_2$" 1 $^1/_2$" x 17 $^1/_2$"
fabric J	1 $^1/_2$" x 14 $^1/_2$" 1 $^1/_2$" x 13 $^1/_2$"	1 $^1/_2$" x 18 $^1/_2$" 1 $^1/_2$" x 19 $^1/_2$"
fabric K	1 $^1/_2$" x 12 $^1/_2$" 1 $^1/_2$" x 11 $^1/_2$"	1 $^1/_2$" x 20 $^1/_2$" 1 $^1/_2$" x 21 $^1/_2$"
fabric L	1 $^1/_2$" x 10 $^1/_2$" 1 $^1/_2$" x 9 $^1/_2$"	1 $^1/_2$" x 22 $^1/_2$" 1 $^1/_2$" x 23 $^1/_2$"
fabric M	1 $^1/_2$" x 8 $^1/_2$" 1 $^1/_2$" x 7 $^1/_2$"	1 $^1/_2$" x 24 $^1/_2$" 1 $^1/_2$" x 25 $^1/_2$"
fabric N	1 $^1/_2$" x 6 $^1/_2$" 1 $^1/_2$" x 5 $^1/_2$"	1 $^1/_2$" x 26 $^1/_2$" 1 $^1/_2$" x 27 $^1/_2$"
fabric O	1 $^1/_2$" x 4 $^1/_2$" 1 $^1/_2$" x 3 $^1/_2$"	1 $^1/_2$" x 28 $^1/_2$" 1 $^1/_2$" x 29 $^1/_2$"
fabric P	1 $^1/_2$" x 2 $^1/_2$" 1 $^1/_2$" x 1 $^1/_2$"	1 $^1/_2$" x 30 $^1/_2$" 1 $^1/_2$" x 31 $^1/_2$"

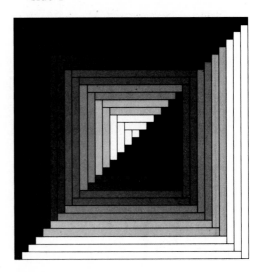

side 1

side 2

Border: Cut 2 strips 2 $^1/_2$" x 32 $^1/_2$" and 2 strips 2 $^1/_2$" x 36 $^1/_2$".

Friends in the Forest (page 62)

Ten-inch Schoolhouse blocks are cut down slightly to fit 9 3/4" log cabin blocks. At this point, Corki doesn't remember how she pieced the border, except that it involved at lot of finagling. I've arrived at a set of measurements that work, but they make a quilt somewhat larger than Corki's.

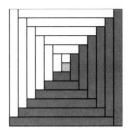

		Fabric required
Quilt size	76 1/2" x 96 1/2"	
Number of blocks	40 log cabin blocks,	3 yards total light green fabrics
	8 Schoolhouse blocks	4 yards total dark green fabrics
Block size	9 3/4" finished	3/4 yard yellow fabric
Log width	3/4" finished	1/4 yard brown fabric
Number of rounds	6	scraps for schoolhouses
Border	pieced (see below)	2 1/4 yards navy starry fabric
		(includes binding)

Cutting instructions

Centers: Cut 40 yellow squares 1 1/4" x 1 1/4".

Light logs: Cut 40 sets from light prints.

1 1/4" x 1 1/4"	1 1/4" x 5 3/4"
1 1/4" x 2"	1 1/4" x 6 1/2"
1 1/4" x 2 3/4"	1 1/4" x 7 1/4"
1 1/4" x 3 1/2"	1 1/4" x 8"
1 1/4" x 4 1/4"	1 1/4" x 8 3/4"
1 1/4" x 5"	1 1/4" x 9 1/2"

Dark logs: Cut 40 sets from dark prints.

1 1/4" x 2"	1 1/4" x 6 1/2"
1 1/4" x 2 3/4"	1 1/4" x 7 1/4"
1 1/4" x 3 1/2"	1 1/4" x 8"
1 1/4" x 4 1/4"	1 1/4" x 8 3/4"
1 1/4" x 5"	1 1/4" x 9 1/2"
1 1/4" x 5 3/4"	1 1/4" x 10 1/4"

Inner border: Strip-piece the inner border of tree trunks and yellow background. Make two 42" strip units, each made from a 1 1/2" cut of brown and a 4 1/2" cut of yellow. Make 52 crosscuts each 1 1/2" wide.

The two side strips are each made from 15 crosscuts sewn together end-to-end. Cut 2 yellow pieces 1 1/2" x 2", and sew one to the yellow end of each strip . Cut 2 yellow pieces 1 1/2" x 5 1/2" and sew them to the top end of each strip (directly to the trunks). Sew to the sides of the quilt.

The top and bottom strips are each made from 11 crosscuts. To lengthen these pieces, add a 1 1/2" x 3 1/4" yellow piece to each yellow end, and a 1 1/2" x 7 1/4" yellow piece to each trunk end. Sew the strips to the top and bottom of the quilt.

Trees: Strip-piece random widths of green fabrics together to make 4 different strip units each 7" wide and 40-42" long. Clean up the left edge of each. Make tick marks every 4 3/4" along one edge of each unit. Starting 2 3/8" in, make tick marks every 4 3/4" along the other edge of each unit. Line up your rotary ruler on the tick marks and cut 15 wedges from each unit, until you have 52.

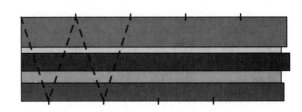

Using the same technique, cut 52 wedges of starry background fabric from 7" wide cuts. Seam the background wedges and tree wedges together to make 15 trees for each side and 11 trees each for the top and bottom. You will need to extend each end of each border strip with a 6 1/2" wide strip of background fabric. After all these wedges it is unlikely that your strips will be mathematically correct, so determine the extensions needed by laying your border strips on the quilt. Sew the completed tree strips to the quilt.

Outer border: Cut 9 strips of the starry border fabric each 2 1/2" wide. Piece 2 strips for the top, 2 for the bottom, and 3 for each of the sides.

The stars in the four corners are about 5" in diameter. Draw them freehand; their charm is in their irregularity. Applique the stars to the corners.

Schoolhouse blocks: For each house, cut the shapes below in the quantities and fabrics listed.

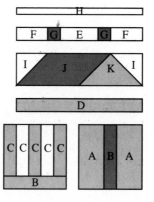
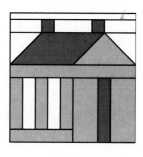

A	2 ¹/₂" x 5 ¹/₂"	2 from house fabric
B	1 ¹/₂" x 5 ¹/₂"	1 from door fabric, 1 from house fabric
C	1 ¹/₂" x 4 ¹/₂"	3 from house fabric, 2 from window fabric
D	1 ¹/₂" x 10 ¹/₂"	1 from house fabric
E	1 ¹/₂" x 3 ¹/₂"	1 from sky fabric
F	1 ¹/₂" x 3"	2 from sky fabric
G	1 ¹/₂" x 1 ¹/₂"	2 from chimney fabric
H	1" x 10 ¹/₂"	1 from sky fabric
I	3 ³/₈" x 3 ³/₈"	1 from sky fabric, cut in half diagonally
J	3" x 8 ³/₄"	1 from roof fabric (trim both ends at 45° angle)
K	6 ¹/₄" x 6 ¹/₄"	1 from house fabric, cut in half diagonally twice (makes 4 roof peaks)

Don and Rachel's Quilt (page 63)

This traditional scrappy quilt uses the machine quilt-as-you-go technique described on page 153. A variety of fabrics were used for the backing squares, and arranged in a symmetrical pattern (page 63). Because there is a lot of waste (I cut 10" squares of backing for 7" log cabin blocks), you need quite a bit of backing fabric.

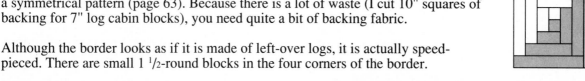

Although the border looks as if it is made of left-over logs, it is actually speed-pieced. There are small 1 ¹/₂-round blocks in the four corners of the border.

		Fabric required
Quilt size	66" x 66"	1 ¹/₂ yards total dark brown fabrics
Number of blocks	64	1 ¹/₂ yards total medium brown fabrics
Block size	7" finished	2 ¹/₂ yards total light brown fabrics
Log width	1" finished	scraps of red fabrics for centers
Number of rounds	3	5 yards total backing fabrics
Border	1" inner border, 4" pieced outer border	5 yards Pellon® ¹/₂ yard binding fabric

Cutting instructions

Follow the measurements for 1" finished logs on page 21, through 6 ¹/₂" light logs and 7 ¹/₂" dark logs.

Centers: Cut 48 from red fabrics and 16 from light-brown fabrics.
Light logs: Cut 16 sets from medium-brown fabrics.
 Cut 48 sets from light-brown fabrics.
Dark logs: Cut 32 sets from dark-brown fabrics.
 Cut 16 sets from medium-brown fabrics.
 Cut 16 sets from light-brown fabrics.

Assemble 16 blocks entirely from light-brown fabrics, 16 blocks entirely from medium-brown fabrics, and 32 blocks from dark-brown fabrics and light-brown fabics.

Inner border: From one light-brown fabric, piece 2 strips 1 ¹/₂" x 56 ¹/₂", and 2 strips 1 ¹/₂" x 58 ¹/₂".

Pieced outer border: Construct strip units from 1 ¹/₂" cuts of dark- and medium-brown fabrics. (You would need, for example, about 3 strips units 40" long, each made up of 10 brown strips.) Crosscut every 4 ¹/₂".

Assemble into four border panels each 58 ¹/₂" long, mixing crosscuts so the border looks scrappy.

Make four corner blocks from red centers and medium-brown fabrics, following the measurements on page 21 through 3 ¹/₂" dark logs and 4 ¹/₂" light logs.
Sew two pieced panels to the top and bottom of the quilt. Sew the corner blocks to the ends of the side panels, then sew them to the sides of the quilt.

Deep Purple Dreams (page 65)

This design is the bare-bones model of Vashon Interweave (page 81). I first made that exceedingly complicated quilt, then calmed the design down to this, which is much simpler to assemble. I puzzled for a while over how to make the interwoven ribbons all the same width without the cornerstones of Vashon Interweave; in Chimneys and Cornerstones blocks, the light and dark halves of the block are equal, unlike the traditional log cabin block. Finally I discovered that piecing the A blocks counterclockwise and the B blocks clockwise does the trick.

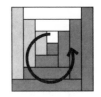

A
(counterclockwise)

B
(clockwise)

Although there are only two blocks, they can be combined in a variety of ways. The simplest repeat design, used for Deep Purple Dreams, is a four-block unit of two A blocks and two B blocks.

Quilt size	50" x 50"
Number of blocks	36
Block size	7" finished
Log width	1" finished
Number of rounds	3
Border	1" inner border, 3" outer border

Fabric required

1 $^1/_4$ yards purple fabrics
1 $^1/_4$ yards blue fabrics
$^1/_2$ yard background fabric
$^1/_4$ yard inner border fabric
$^2/_3$ yard outer border fabric
2 $^1/_2$ yards backing fabric
$^1/_2$ yard binding fabric

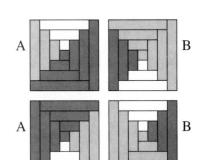

4-block unit

Cutting instructions

Centers: Cut 1 $^1/_2$" x 1 $^1/_2$" squares, 18 from a variety of purple fabrics and 18 from a variety of blue fabrics.

Background logs: Cut 36 sets from the background fabric.
　　1 $^1/_2$" x 1 $^1/_2$"
　　1 $^1/_2$" x 3 $^1/_2$"
　　1 $^1/_2$" x 5 $^1/_2$"

Purple logs: Cut 18 sets from a variety of fabrics.
　　1 $^1/_2$" x 2 $^1/_2$"
　　1 $^1/_2$" x 4 $^1/_2$"
　　1 $^1/_2$" x 6 $^1/_2$"
Cut another 18 sets from a variety of fabrics, following the measurements for 1" finished logs on page 21, through 7 $^1/_2$".

Blue logs: Follow the instructions for purple logs.

Piece 18 A blocks and 18 B blocks, following the diagrams above.

Inner border: Cut 2 strips 1 $^1/_2$" x 42 $^1/_2$" and piece 2 strips 1 $^1/_2$" x 44 $^1/_2$".

Outer border: Piece 2 strips 3 $^1/_2$" x 44 $^1/_2$" and 2 strips 3 $^1/_2$" x 50 $^1/_2$".

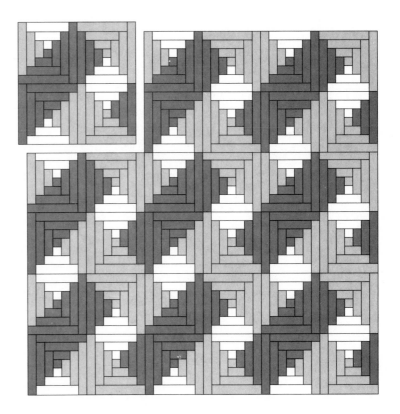

An eight-block unit of four A and four B blocks makes a staggered two over, two under design. The quilt shown requires eight 8-block units.

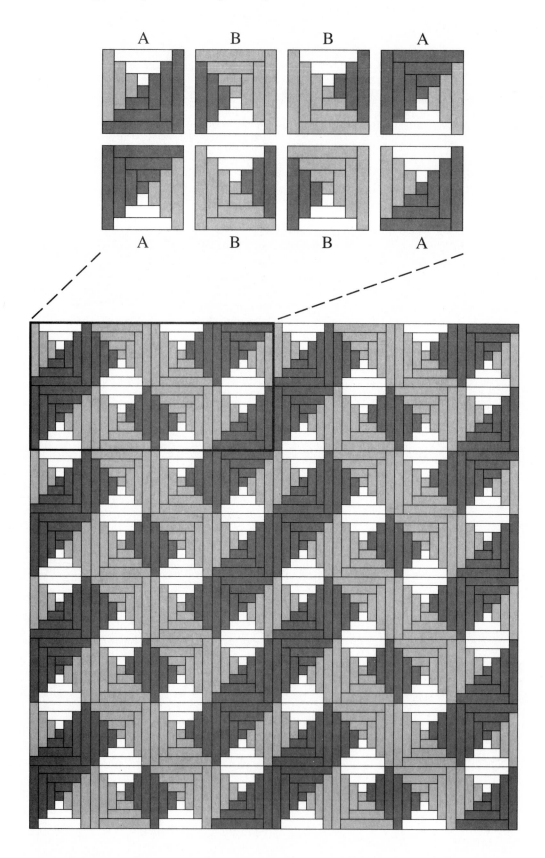

A B B A

A B B A

Vashon Interweave uses a 16-block unit of eight A and eight B blocks
to make a design in which pairs of ribbons weave two over, two under.
The quilt shown requires four 16-block units.

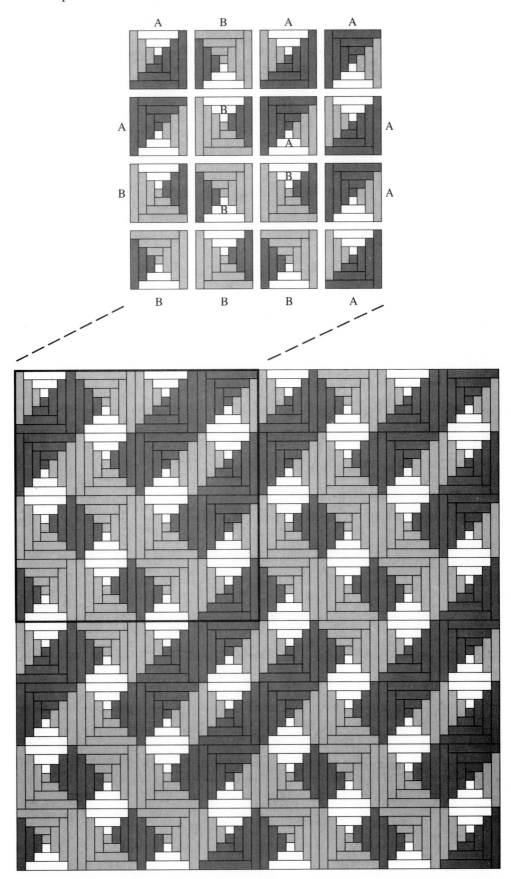

Rectangular and square log cabin blocks can be combined to create new designs.

Rectangular Log Cabins

Any log cabin block can be made rectangular instead of square, by starting with a rectangular center.

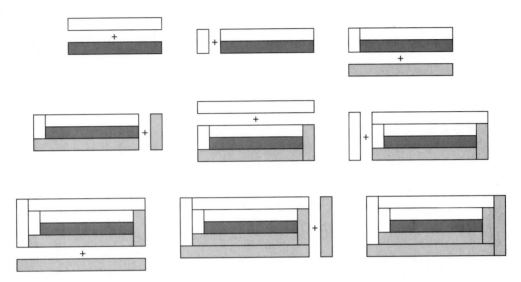

If you have ever crocheted an oval rag rug or woven an oval basket, you know that as you add to a long shape in rounds, equally to all sides, the shape becomes less and less elongated.

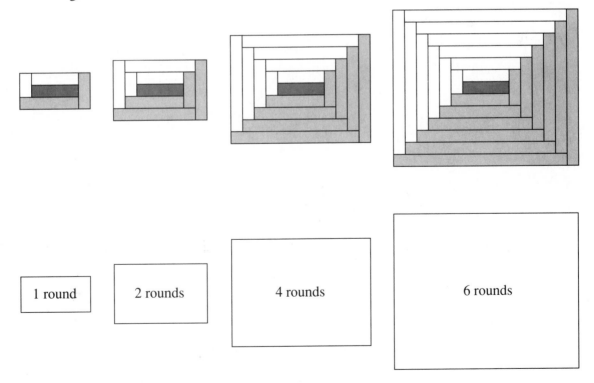

You must start with a very long center piece to achieve a distinctly rectangular log cabin block, and the more rounds you plan to add the more elongated your center must be. For example, if you want to make a three-round rectangular log cabin block that is twice as long as it is wide, you cannot start with a center that is twice as long as it is wide.

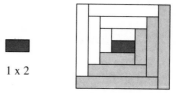

1 x 2

7 x 8

To make a three-round block that is twice as long as it is wide, you must start with a center that is eight times as long as it is wide.

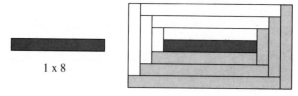

1 x 8

7 x 14

It must be possible to figure out the mathematics involved, but I have never bothered; I just sketch until I arrive at a block with proportions that please me. I have provided the log measurements for the rectangular quilts in this book; they will give you a starting point from which to design your own quilts.

Rectangular blocks, of course, elongate the overall design of the quilt. Below is a rectangular Barn Raising.

You might want to experiment with combinations of rectangular and square blocks. It is easiest to use rectangular blocks that are an even multiple of the measurements of the square block; for example, the same width and twice as long as the square block. See the diagram on page 32.

Construction Techniques

A rectangular log cabin block, just as a square log cabin block, can be turned into four positions. The mirror image of the rectangular block can be turned into four *different* positions. Look at these two rows of rectangular blocks. Each block in row B is the mirror image of the block just above it in row A. There is no way you can rotate one of the blocks in row A to make it identical to a block in row B.

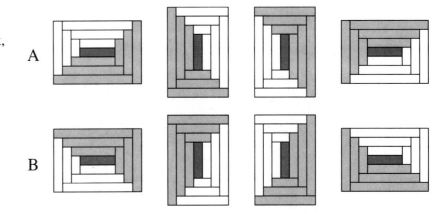

There are, then, eight positions for rectangular log cabin blocks. Your particular quilt design might use one or several or all eight. Sketch your rectangular quilt. Compare each block in your sketch to the blocks above, and label all blocks A or B. Total up the number of each you will need to make. In the Barn-Raising quilt on page 34, for example, there are 18 A blocks and 18 B blocks.

In the illustrations of A and B blocks above, the B blocks are drawn as actual mirror images of the A blocks. The A blocks are constructed counterclockwise, and the B blocks are constructed clockwise. Even though you would generally not mix the two types of construction in a log cabin quilt, it saves a lot of time with rectangular blocks. If you construct all the blocks counterclockwise, you must work from two sets of measurements, and two sets of logs.

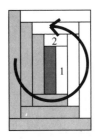 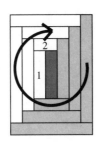 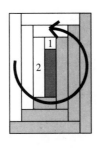

A counterclockwise   B clockwise   B counterclockwise

For example, look at these three blocks. In the two counterclockwise blocks, logs 1 and 2 are not the same. In fact, none of the logs are. If, however, you construct the A blocks counterclockwise and the B blocks clockwise, you can use the same log measurements for both types of blocks.

The two B blocks look different here because you can see all the seamlines clearly. The difference would not be noticeable in a quilt.

To keep confusion at a minimum, sew all of the counterclockwise blocks first, then all of the clockwise. You must keep your wits about you for the first few logs, but then you can be guided, as with the basic log cabin block, by (1) which side of the block has two seams, and (2) whether that side is dark or light. At each step, only one log will fit.

> **If your rectangular quilt is a combination of A and B blocks, construct the A blocks counterclockwise and the B blocks clockwise.**

Big City Blues; *color plate on page 65, instructions on page 37.*

Instructions: Rectangular Log Cabins

Persia (page 66)

The smaller portion of each block is solid purple. For each color combination, sew half of the blocks clockwise and half counterclockwise.

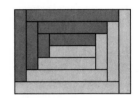

Quilt size	48" x 66"	**Fabric required**	
Number of blocks	4 green/purple,	1 $3/4$ yards purple fabric	
	20 print/purple,	1 $1/2$ yards green fabric	
	12 lavender/purple (36 total)	(includes border and	
Block size	7" x 10" finished	binding)	
Log width	1" finished	1 $1/4$ yards multicolor	
Number of rounds	3	fabric	
Border	3"	$3/4$ yard lavender fabric	
		3 yards backing fabric	

Cutting instructions

Purple logs: Cut 36 sets. Note that two of the measurements repeat; they are listed separately to indicate the order in which the logs are added to the block.

1 $1/2$" x 4 $1/2$"	1 $1/2$" x 4 $1/2$"
1 $1/2$" x 2 $1/2$"	1 $1/2$" x 8 $1/2$"
1 $1/2$" x 6 $1/2$"	1 $1/2$" x 6 $1/2$"

Green, multicolor, and lavender logs: Cut 4 sets from green, 20 sets from the print, and 12 sets from lavender.

1 $1/2$" x 4 $1/2$" (center)	1 $1/2$" x 7 $1/2$"
1 $1/2$" x 5 $1/2$"	1 $1/2$" x 5 $1/2$"
1 $1/2$" x 3 $1/2$"	1 $1/2$" x 9 $1/2$"
	1 $1/2$" x 7 $1/2$"

Border: Cut 2 strips 3 $1/2$" x 42 $1/2$" and piece 2 strips 3 $1/2$" x 66 $1/2$".

Big City Blues (page 65; diagram opposite)

You have to look closely at this quilt to see that it is a traditional Streak o' Lightning design; the design is more evident in the diagram on the facing page. Moving from the top of the quilt to the bottom (from the light end to the dark end), each of the four horizontal rows of blocks is a different combination of colors: light/light-medium, light-medium/medium, medium/medium-dark, medium dark/dark.

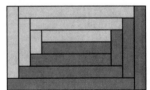

Quilt size	50" x 56"	**Fabric required**	
Number of blocks	24	$1/2$ yard total light fabrics	
Block size	7" x 12" finished	$3/4$ yard total light-medium fabrics	
Log width	1" finished	$3/4$ yard total medium fabrics	
Center	1" x 6"	$3/4$ yard total medium-dark fabrics	
Number of rounds	3	$1/2$ yard total dark fabrics	
Border	4"	1 yard border fabric	
		2 $1/2$ yards backing fabric	
		$1/2$ yard binding fabric	

Cutting instructions

NOTE: The larger portion of each block is always the darker color group. Sew half of the blocks clockwise and half counterclockwise.

Light logs: Cut 6 sets in each of 4 color groups (light, light-medium, medium, medium-dark). The logs are listed in the order in which they are added to the block.

1 $1/2$" x 6 $1/2$"	1 $1/2$" x 4 $1/2$"
1 $1/2$" x 2 $1/2$"	1 $1/2$" x 10 $1/2$"
1 $1/2$" x 8 $1/2$"	1 $1/2$" x 6 $1/2$"

Dark logs: Cut 6 sets in each of 4 color groups (light-medium, medium, medium-dark, dark).

1 $1/2$" x 6 $1/2$" (center)	1 $1/2$" x 5 $1/2$"
1 $1/2$" x 7 $1/2$"	1 $1/2$" x 11 $1/2$"
1 $1/2$" x 3 $1/2$"	1 $1/2$" x 7 $1/2$"
1 $1/2$" x 9 $1/2$"	

Border: Cut 2 strips 4 $1/2$" x 42 $1/2$" and piece 2 strips 4 $1/2$" x 56 $1/2$".

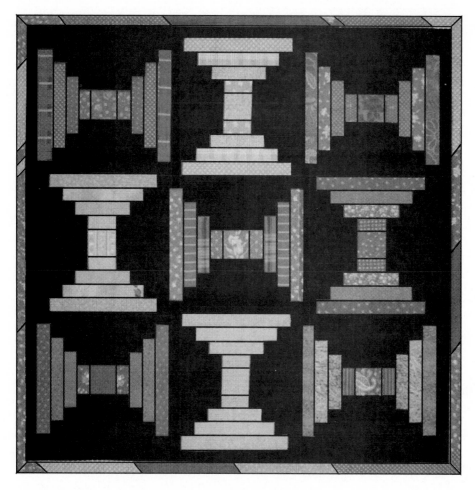

Scrappy Spools; *color plate on page 67, instructions on page 42.*

Courthouse Steps

Courthouse Steps is an old version of log cabin. The block also starts with a center square, to which light and dark logs are added in the order two light, two dark, two light, and so on. Instead of adding the logs in a spiral out from the center, however, each pair of logs is added to opposite sides of the center.

If you find it annoying to press your log cabin block after each log is added, Courthouse Steps is the variation for you; you can add two logs to each block before you must press.

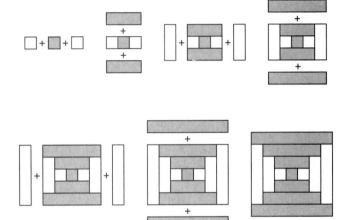

In the traditional Courthouse Steps block, lights and darks are added in pairs so that the block is made up of two opposite dark triangles and two opposite light triangles.

Where the regular log cabin block has four positions and the rectangular block eight, the traditional Courthouse Steps block has only two possible positions.

There are two traditional Courthouse Steps layouts, which I call Beads and Spools.

Beads Layout

Spools Layout

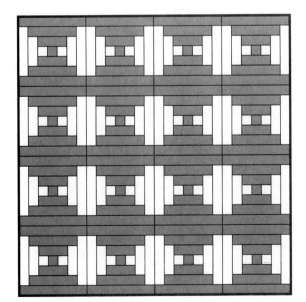
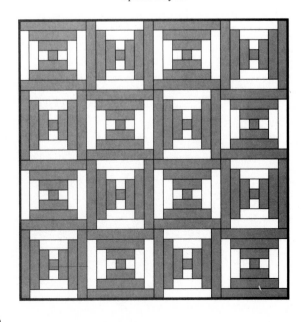

The Courthouse Steps block divides easily into four triangles. Try different color placements to develop interesting overall designs.

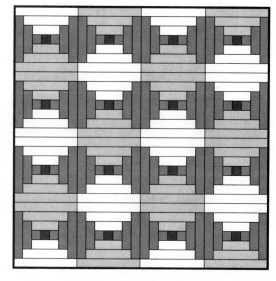

Block Construction

There is nothing exotic about the Courthouse Steps block; just remember to press thoroughly after each pair of logs is added. Always press toward the new logs.

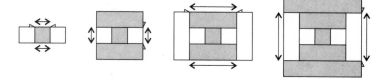

A spindly center (as in Scrappy Spools, page 67) results when the center matches the first pair of logs. For a balanced block, the center should match the *second* pair of logs added. For example, if you have a dark center and want a balanced block, start with a pair of light logs.

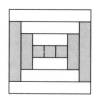 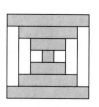

spindly center   balanced block

Spiral Courthouse Steps   In the traditional Courthouse Steps block, logs are added in dark/dark, light/light pairs to opposite sides of the block. If the logs are added in dark/light pairs, a spiral design develops. If you start the block as shown, with two small squares, add only one of the last pair of logs to make the block square.

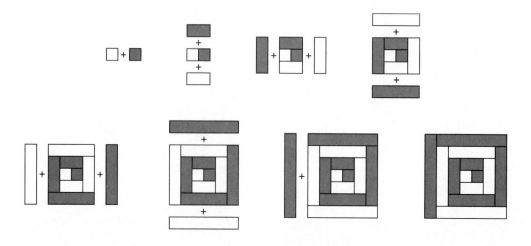

Instructions: Courthouse Steps

Old-Fashioned Courthouse Steps (page 68)

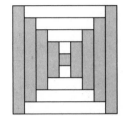

This is a very traditional, scrappy Courthouse Steps in the Spool layout. For the border, long strips are added as if the body of the quilt were the center of a big Courthouse Steps block: two dark strips to opposite sides, then two light strips to the other sides, and so on. If you choose a planned arrangement of fabrics rather than scrappy, you can speed-piece the center and the first two light logs (page 19).

		Fabric required
Quilt size	53" x 53"	2 yards total dark fabrics
Number of blocks	25	2 yards total light fabrics
Block size	9" finished	2 $1/4$ yards backing fabric
Log width	1" finished	$1/2$ yard binding fabric
Number of rounds	4	
Border	4 strips each 1" wide	

Cutting instructions

Centers: Cut 25 squares 1 $1/2$" x 1 $1/2$".

Dark logs: Cut 50 sets.
  1 $1/2$" x 3 $1/2$"
  1 $1/2$" x 5 $1/2$"
  1 $1/2$" x 7 $1/2$"
  1 $1/2$" x 9 $1/2$"

Light logs: Cut 50 sets.
  1 $1/2$" x 1 $1/2$"
  1 $1/2$" x 3 $1/2$"
  1 $1/2$" x 5 $1/2$"
  1 $1/2$" x 7 $1/2$"

Border: Piece strips as indicated. Add in the order listed, lights on two opposite sides and darks on the other sides.

  1 $1/2$" x 45 $1/2$" 2 light
  1 $1/2$" x 47 $1/2$" 2 dark, 2 light
  1 $1/2$" x 49 $1/2$" 2 dark, 2 light
  1 $1/2$" x 51 $1/2$" 2 dark, 2 light
  1 $1/2$" x 53 $1/2$" 2 dark

Shaded Placemats (page 69)

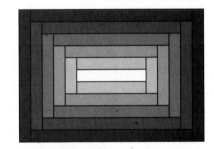

Each placemat is a single rectangular Courthouse Steps block, in a shaded series of fabrics. Use the machine quilt-as-you-go method described on page 153. The binding is 1" wide finished, so that it looks like the final round of logs.

Quilt size	13" x 18"
Number of blocks	one per placemat
Block size	11" x 16" finished
Log width	1" finished
Number of rounds	5

Cutting instructions

Centers: Cut 4 strips 1 $1/2$" x 6 $1/2$" from fabric A.
Logs: Cut 8 sets from the fabrics listed. The logs are listed in the same order they are added to the block.

fabric B	1 $1/2$" x 6 $1/2$"
fabric B	1 $1/2$" x 3 $1/2$"
fabric C	1 $1/2$" x 8 $1/2$"
fabric C	1 $1/2$" x 5 $1/2$"
fabric D	1 $1/2$" x 10 $1/2$"
fabric D	1 $1/2$" x 7 $1/2$"
fabric E	1 $1/2$" x 12 $1/2$"
fabric E	1 $1/2$" x 9 $1/2$"
fabric F	1 $1/2$" x 14 $1/2$"
fabric F	1 $1/2$" x 11 $1/2$"

Fabric required for four identical placemats
  $1/8$ yard fabric A (lightest)
  $1/4$ yard fabrics B, C, and D
  $1/3$ yard fabric E
  $1/2$ yard fabric F
  $3/4$ yard fabric G (darkest) for binding
  1 yard Pellon®
  1 yard backing fabric

Batting and backing: Cut 4 pieces of each 16" x 22". After assembling the block on the batting and backing, trim so that batting and backing extend $3/4$" beyond the raw edges of the block.

Binding: Cut 7 strips each 2 $3/4$" x 42" and sew together end-to-end for single-fold binding that finishes 1" wide. See page 153 for binding instructions.

Scrappy Spools (page 67; diagram on page 38)

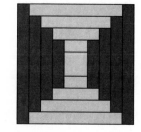

The blocks for this quilt were constructed using the machine quilt-as-you-go technique; see page 153. After the blocks were joined, I decided not to hand-finish the back. Instead, I simply laid the top on the backing, basted around the edges, and added the binding. This covered the raw edges on the back, and since the quilt is a wall hanging it doesn't matter that the backing is attached to the quilt only at the edges.

		Fabric required
Quilt size	40" x 40"	1 1/2 yard black fabric
Number of blocks	9	scraps of various fabrics in
Block size	12 1/2" finished	9 different colors (includes binding)
Log width	1 1/4" finished	1 1/2 yards backing fabric
Number of rounds	4	

Cutting instructions
Centers: Cut one square 3" x 3" in each of the 9 different colors.
Color logs: Cut 2 sets from one fabric, for each of the 9 colors (= 18 sets).

1 3/4" x 3"	*Black logs:* Cut 18 sets.
1 3/4" x 5 1/2"	1 3/4" x 5 1/2"
1 3/4" x 8"	1 3/4" x 8"
1 3/4" x 10 1/2"	1 3/4" x 10 1/2"
	1 3/4" x 13"

Binding: Cut 10" x 3 1/4" pieces of a variety of prints; sew together with diagonal seams. Trim the outer edges of the quilt so the backing and batting extend 1" beyond the raw edges of the quilt top, for binding that finishes 1 1/4" wide. See page 153.

Yellow Spools (page 70; diagram on page 140)

Sashing strips, unusual in log cabin quilts, are used here to isolate the Courthouse Steps Spool blocks. The border includes both regular log cabin and Courthouse Steps blocks.

Quilt size	71" x 71"
Number of blocks	9 Spool blocks, 28 log cabin blocks, 4 Courthouse Steps blocks
Block size	13" finished Spool blocks, 7" finished border blocks
Log width	1" finished
Number of rounds	3
Sashing	2", 2" x 2" yellow set blocks
Border	3" inner border, 7" pieced border, 4" outer border

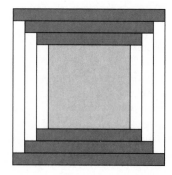

Fabric required
1/4 yard each of 9 yellow fabrics
1 1/2 yards total of 8 or more medium brown fabrics
1 3/4 yards background fabric, including sashing and inner border
1 yard outer border fabric
4 1/2 yards backing fabric
1/2 yard binding fabric

Cutting Instructions
NOTE: The inner border strips and the background logs are cut from the same fabric. Cut the inner border strips first, cutting them parallel to the selvages so you won't have to piece them.

SPOOL BLOCKS
Centers: Cut 9 from different yellows, 7 1/2" x 7 1/2".
Dark logs: Cut 18 sets from a variety of browns.   *Light logs:* Cut 18 sets from background fabric.

1 1/2" x 9 1/2"	1 1/2" x 7 1/2"
1 1/2" x 11 1/2"	1 1/2" x 9 1/2"
1 1/2" x 13 1/2"	1 1/2" x 11 1/2"

SASHING AND BORDERS

Sashing strips: Cut 12 pieces 2 ¹/₂" x 13 ¹/₂" from background fabric.
Set blocks: Cut 4 squares 2 ¹/₂" x 2 ¹/₂" from 4 yellow fabrics.
Inner border: Cut 2 strips 3 ¹/₂" x 43 ¹/₂" and 2 strips 3 ¹/₂" x 49 ¹/₂" from
    background fabric. If you cut these before you cut the background logs, you can
    cut them parallel to the selvages and avoid piecing them.
Outer border: Piece 2 strips 4 ¹/₂" x 63 ¹/₂", and 2 strips 4 ¹/₂" x 71 ¹/₂".

Border blocks

PIECED BORDER BLOCKS

Piece 28 log cabin blocks and 4 Courthouse Steps blocks.

Light logs: Cut the number indicated from background fabric.

36	1 ¹/₂" x 1 ¹/₂"
28	1 ¹/₂" x 2 ¹/₂"
40	1 ¹/₂" x 3 ¹/₂"
28	1 ¹/₂" x 4 ¹/₂"
40	1 ¹/₂" x 5 ¹/₂"
28	1 ¹/₂" x 6 ¹/₂"
4	1 ¹/₂" x 7 ¹/₂"

log cabin

Dark logs: Cut the number indicated from a variety of browns.

32	1 ¹/₂" x 1 ¹/₂" (centers)
28	1 ¹/₂" x 2 ¹/₂"
32	1 ¹/₂" x 3 ¹/₂"
28	1 ¹/₂" x 4 ¹/₂"
32	1 ¹/₂" x 5 ¹/₂"
28	1 ¹/₂" x 6 ¹/₂"
32	1 ¹/₂" x 7 ¹/₂"

Courthouse Steps

Amish Spools (page 67)

The Spool block from the Yellow Spools quilt was scaled down here for a wall hanging.

Quilt size	32" x 32"
Number of blocks	9
Block size	6 ¹/₂" finished
Log width	¹/₂" finished
Number of rounds	3
Sashing	1"
Border	1" accent border, 3" outer border

Fabric required

¹/₄ yards or scraps of solid-color fabrics,
    in dark + light pairs for 9 blocks
1 ¹/₂ yards black fabric (includes sashing and
    outer border)
1 yard backing fabric
¹/₂ yard binding fabric

Cutting instructions

Centers: Cut 9 squares 4" x 4".
"Spool" logs: Cut 2 sets for each spool block = 18 sets.
    1" x 5"
    1" x 6"
    1" x 7"
Background logs: Cut 18 sets from black.
    1" x 4"
    1" x 5"
    1" x 6"

Sashing: Cut 6 strips 1 ¹/₂" x 7" and 2 strips 1 ¹/₂" x 22" from black.
Inner border: Cut 2 strips 1 ¹/₂" x 22" and 2 strips 1 ¹/₂" x 24" from black.
Accent border: Cut 2 strips 1 ¹/₂" x 24" and 2 strips 1 ¹/₂" x 26" from one of the solid colors.
Outer border: Cut 2 strips 3 ¹/₂" x 26" and 2 strips 3 ¹/₂" x 32" from black.

Courthouse Stars (page 69)

With its large unpieced squares and rectangles, this quilt top that can be quickly assembled. Use an active print for the unpieced background areas, as Karen did, or use a solid fabric and fill it with hand quilting.

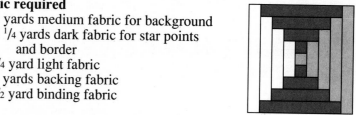

Quilt size	62" x 62"
Number of blocks	16
Block size	9" finished
Log width	1" finished
Number of rounds	4
Border	4"

Fabric required
2 yards medium fabric for background
2 1/4 yards dark fabric for star points and border
3/4 yard light fabric
4 yards backing fabric
1/2 yard binding fabric

Cutting instructions
Speed piece the centers and the first pair of dark logs. Make 1 1/2 strip units from 1 1/2"-wide selvage-to-selvage cuts of medium background fabric and dark fabric, as illustrated. Press seam allowances toward the dark fabric strips. Make 32 crosscuts each 1 1/2" wide.

Dark logs: Cut 32 sets from dark fabric.
  1 1/2" x 3 1/2"
  1 1/2" x 5 1/2"
  1 1/2" x 7 1/2"

Medium logs: Cut 16 sets from medium background fabric.
  1 1/2" x 3 1/2"
  1 1/2" x 5 1/2"
  1 1/2" x 7 1/2"
  1 1/2" x 9 1/2"

Light logs: Cut 16 sets from light fabric.
  1 1/2" x 3 1/2"
  1 1/2" x 5 1/2"
  1 1/2" x 7 1/2"
  1 1/2" x 9 1/2"

Border strips: Piece 2 strips 4 1/2" x 54 1/2" and 2 strips 4 1/2" x 62 1/2".

Fish Maze (page 68)

This pillow top is made of four small Spiral Courthouse Steps blocks with sashing strips to complete the design. Use a pillow form in a size slightly larger than the cover for a plump and smooth pillow.

Pillow size	17" x 17"
Number of blocks	4
Block size	5" finished
Log width	1" finished
Border	1" sashing strips and inner border; 2" outer border (or as desired)

Fabric required
1/4 yard light fabric
3/4 yard dark fabric (includes pillow back)
18" pillow form

Cutting instructions
NOTE: Cut your pillow back first, then the pillow border. Cut the logs from the remaining fabric.

Logs: Cut 4 sets from dark and 4 from light.
  1 1/2" x 1 1/2" (center)
  1 1/2" x 2 1/2"
  1 1/2" x 3 1/2"
  1 1/2" x 4 1/2"
  1 1/2" x 5 1/2" (cut 4 dark only)
Piece the blocks as illustrated; piece 2 of A and 2 of B.

Sashing: From light cut 2 strips 1 1/2" x 5 1/2". From dark cut one strip 1 1/2" x 11 1/2".

Inner border: From light cut 2 strips 1 1/2" x 11 1/2" and 2 strips 1 1/2" x 13 1/2".

Outer border: From dark cut 2 strips 2 1/2" x 13 1/2" and 2 strips 2 1/2" x 17 1/2".

Under the Sea (page 71)

A shaded collection of hand-dyed fabrics and an irregularly dyed green fabric suggest underwater lighting, and Spiral Courthouse Steps blocks suggest waves and currents. An irregular piece of a vivid tropical fish print forms the bottom of the quilt, and overlaps some of the Courthouse Steps blocks. Joan cut individual fish from the printed fabric and machine-stitched them to the quilt top; these and the large piece of fish fabric were machine-stitched on with the edges left unfinished. She then put the quilt top through the washer and dryer to fray the raw edges for a feathery look.

Quilt size   40" x 56"
Number of blocks 16
Block size   8 3/4" x 10" finished
Log width   1 1/4" finished
Border   1 1/2"

Fabric required
packet of hand-dyed 1/8 yard pieces, or 1/8 yard each of 6 to 8 solid greens
3/4 yard light green fabric
approximately 1 1/2 yards tropical fish print fabric
1 3/4 yards backing fabric
1/2 yard binding fabric

Cutting instructions

Logs: Cut one set from dark and one set from light for each of the 16 blocks.

    1 3/4" x 1 3/4" (center)
    1 3/4" x 3"
    1 3/4" x 4 1/4"
    1 3/4" x 5 1/2"
    1 3/4" x 6 3/4"
    1 3/4" x 8"
    1 3/4" x 9 1/2"

The last two strips are added to the same side of the block, instead of opposite sides.

To finish the first three rows of blocks, cut 3 pieces 7 1/2" x 9 1/4" from the light green, and add them to alternate ends of the rows.

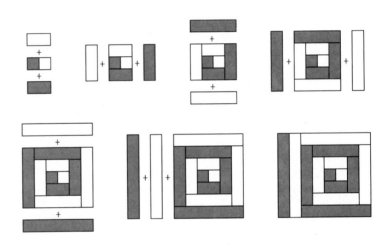

Border: Cut 3 strips 2" x 42". Sew to the top of the quilt and to the sides; they will extend only partway down the sides. Overlap the blocks and border with fish fabric.

Stars and Spirals (page 73)

There is a lot of piecing packed into this small wall hanging; the logs in the Spiral Courthouse Steps blocks are only 1/2" fnished. You can substitute any 8" and 16" pieced or appliqued blocks for the stars.

Quilt size   27" x 26"
Blocks   8 Courthouse Steps,
            5 stars 4" square,
            1 star 8" square
Log width   1/2" finished
Border   3 inner borders each 1/2",
            3" outer border

Fabric required
1/2 yard dark fabric
1/2 yard light fabric
scraps of a variety of fabrics for stars
1/8 yard each dark, medium, and light fabrics for inner borders
1/2 yard fabric for outer border
1 yard backing fabric
1/4 yard binding fabric

Cutting instructions
SPIRAL COURTHOUSE STEPS
Light and dark logs: Cut 8 light and 8 dark sets, except as noted.

    1" x 1" (center)   1" x 3 1/2"
    1" x 1 1/2"   1" x 4"
    1" x 2"   1" x 4 1/2" cut 8 dark, and 4 light for X blocks
    1" x 2 1/2"   1" x 5"   cut only 4 light, for Y blocks
    1" x 3"

In this quilt there are actually two different Spiral Courthouse Steps blocks, X and Y. Both start with the same core block; piece 4 as shown here and 4 mirror images.

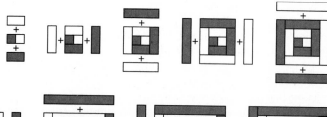

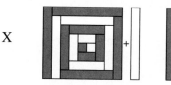

Make 4 X blocks, 2 as shown here and 2 mirror images (X-reversed = Xr). Repeat for the Y blocks; make 2 as shown here and 2 mirror images. The finished size of the X blocks is 5" x 4" (5 ¹/₂" x 4 ¹/₂", including seam allowances). The finished size of the Y blocks is 4 ¹/₂" square (5" square, including seam allowances).

X

Y

STAR BLOCKS

Small sawtooth stars: Piece 5 from scraps (4" square finished).
    Cut 5 squares 2 ¹/₂" x 2 ¹/₂" for the star centers.
    Cut 40 triangles for star points, by cutting 20 squares 1 ⁷/₈"
        x 1 ⁷/₈" and cutting them in half diagonally. In the same
        manner, cut 40 triangles for background.
    Cut 20 squares 1 ¹/₂" x 1 ¹/₂" for background.
One of the 5 small sawtooth star blocks is the center of the large central star.

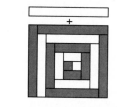

Central Star (8" square finished)
    Cut 8 triangles by cutting 4 squares 2 ⁷/₈" x
      2 ⁷/₈" and cutting them in half diagonally.
    In the same manner, cut another 8 triangles
    for background.
    Cut 4 squares 2 ¹/₂" x 2 ¹/₂" for background.

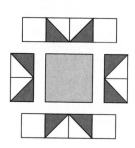

Add light sashing strips around the large central star block, to bring the 8" square block up to the desired size of 9" square (9 ¹/₂", including seam allowances). Cut 2 strips 1" x 8 ¹/₂" and 2 strips 1" x 9 ¹/₂", and add as shown in the diagram.

BORDERS

Inner borders: Cut 4 strips 1" x 18 ¹/₂", 4 strips 1" x 19 ¹/₂", and 4 strips 1" x 20 ¹/₂".
Outer border: Cut 2 strips 3 ¹/₂" x 20 ¹/₂" and 2 strips 3 ¹/₂" x 26 ¹/₂".

Spiral Placemats (page 70)

This is a rectangular, machine quilt-as-you-go version of the Spiral Courthouse Steps block. There are a few modifications in the piecing order so that the dark spiral is entirely enclosed in background fabric. See page 153 for machine quilt-as-you-go directions.

Quilt size	13" x 19"
Number of blocks	1 per placemat
Block size	12" x 18" finished
Log width	1" finished, 1" x 7" centers
Number of rounds	5 ¹/₂

Fabric required for four placemats
- 1 ¹/₂ yards design fabric (includes binding)
- ³/₄ yards background fabric
- 1 yard backing fabric
- 1 yard Pellon®

Cutting instructions

Centers: Cut 4 strips 1 ¹/₂" x 6 ¹/₂" from background fabric, and 4 squares 1 ¹/₂" x 1 ¹/₂" from the design fabric. Piece the centers.

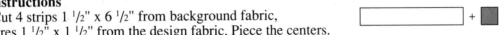

Logs: Cut 4 sets from the design fabric and 4 sets from the background fabric, except as noted. The logs are listed in the order they are added to the block.

1 ¹/₂" x 7 ¹/₂"	1 ¹/₂" x 15 ¹/₂"	cut 4 from design fabric only
1 ¹/₂" x 3 ¹/₂"	1 ¹/₂" x 10 ¹/₂"	
1 ¹/₂" x 9 ¹/₂"	1 ¹/₂" x 17 ¹/₂"	cut 8 from background fabric only
1 ¹/₂" x 5 ¹/₂"	1 ¹/₂" x 12 ¹/₂"	cut 4 from background fabric only
1 ¹/₂" x 11 ¹/₂"		
1 ¹/₂" x 7 ¹/₂"		
1 ¹/₂" x 13 ¹/₂"		
1 ¹/₂" x 9 ¹/₂"		

Follow directions for Spiral Courthouse Steps (page 40) through the second pair of 9 ¹/₂" logs (the left column above). Then proceed as shown below with the logs in the right column.

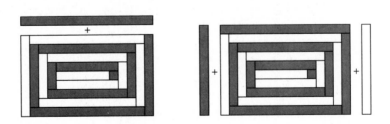

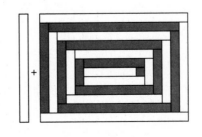

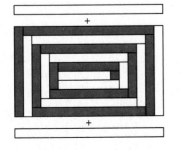

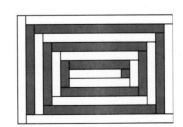

Purple Mums; *color plate on page 74, instructions on page 58.*

Off-Center Log Cabins

The off-center log cabin is my favorite variation. The blocks are simple to construct but the design possibilities are tantalizing. Many effects difficult to achieve with regular log cabin blocks are possible with off-center blocks.

The basic off-center block starts with a square, and logs are added alternately to only two sides of the square. The "center" then ends up in a corner of the block.

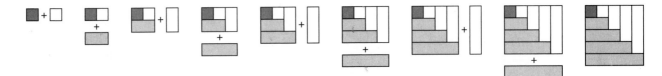

Like the traditional log cabin block, the off-center block can be thought of as a square composed of two triangles.

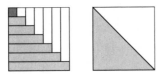

Like the traditional log cabin block, the off-center block can be rotated into four positions.

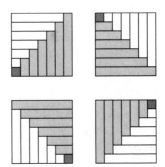

All of the logs in the dark (or light) area are parallel. This adds an interesting difference to any of the traditional log cabin designs. Linear prints can be emphasized, as in the quilt Watercolor on page 72.

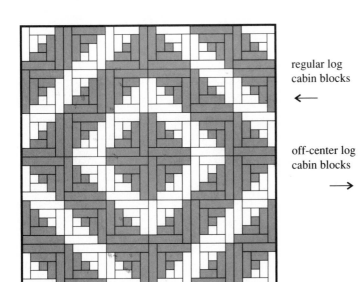

regular log
cabin blocks

←

off-center log
cabin blocks

→

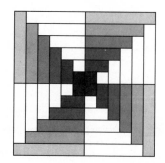

Shaded off-center blocks are particularly effective, as in Green Pinwheels (page 75).

It isn't necessary to divide off-center blocks into light and dark halves. You can instead add the logs in identical pairs, making a chevron shape, and then set the blocks on point. The striking quilt Rhapsody in Blue (page 73) is made of simple shaded off-center blocks.

Cabin Rose (page 76) is one of the first log cabin variations I designed. The block is a simple off-center log cabin, but one of the logs is strip-pieced to make the stem.

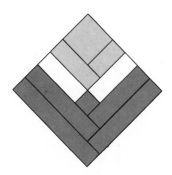

The block can easily be expanded or contracted, and the leaves can be shortened or shaped by strip-piecing. The quilt Spring Flowers (page 74) is the most simplified version.

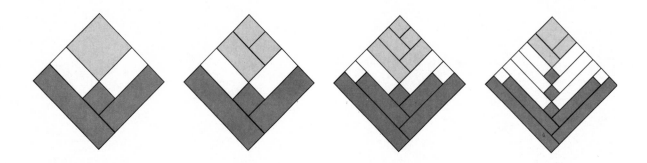

For a rather loopy version of the off-center log cabin, try adding one or two full rounds of logs to an off-center block, embedding the center square.

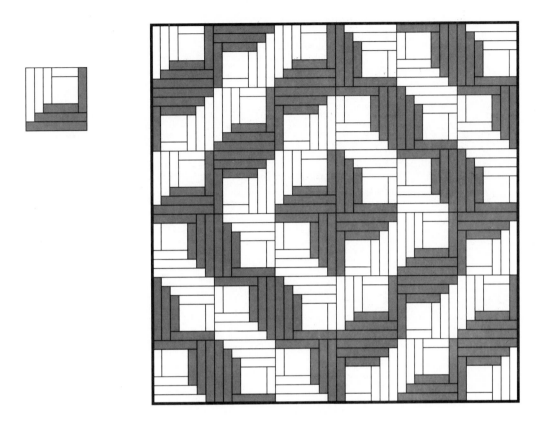

Block construction

Off-center log cabins are even easier to sew than regular log cabins, because there is less chance to be confused about where to put the next log. Just keep adding logs alternately to two adjoining sides of the "center."

As with the regular log cabin block, press after each log is added and press all seam allowances toward the log just added.

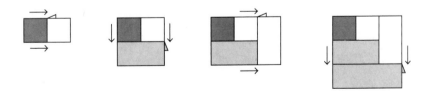

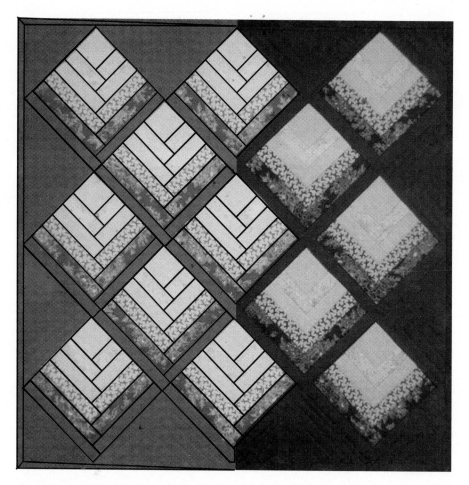

Rhapsody in Blue *by Marie Blichfeldt; color plate on page 73, instructions on page 53.*

Instructions: Off-Center Log Cabins

Rhapsody in Blue (page 73)

Vibrant blues shading to black make a striking wall quilt. Each new fabric is added as a pair of logs, chevron-style. The final round looks like sashing strips when the blocks are assembled. For diagonal set instructions, see page 150.

		Fabric required
Quilt size	40" x 40"	$1/8$ yard fabric A (lightest)
Number of blocks	13	$1/4$ yard each fabrics B, C, D
Block size	8 $3/4$" finished	$1/2$ yard fabric E
Log width	1 $1/4$"	1 yard fabric F (includes edge triangles)
Number of rounds	5	1 $1/2$ yards backing fabric
		$1/2$ yard binding fabric

Cutting instructions

Centers: Cut 13 squares 3" x 3" from fabric A (lightest).
Logs: Cut 13 of each pair from the fabric listed.

1 $3/4$" x 3"	fabric B	1 $3/4$" x 6 $3/4$"	fabric D
1 $3/4$" x 4 $1/4$"	fabric B	1 $3/4$" x 6 $3/4$"	fabric E
1 $3/4$" x 4 $1/4$"	fabric C	1 $3/4$" x 8"	fabric E
1 $3/4$" x 5 $1/2$"	fabric C	1 $3/4$" x 8"	fabric F
1 $3/4$" x 5 $1/2$"	fabric D	1 $3/4$" x 9 $1/4$"	fabric F

Edge triangles: Cut from fabric F.
   Cut 4 squares 9 $5/8$" x 9 $5/8$" and cut in half diagonally to make 8 triangles for the edges.
   Cut a square 10" x 10" and cut in half diagonally twice to make 4 triangles for the corners.

Green Pinwheels (page 75)

Select your fabrics carefully to make a regular series shaded from dark to light. As with any traditional pinwheel design the pinwheels overlap, but here there are two different types: some of them have dark centers, and some light centers.

		Fabric required
Quilt size	50" x 50"	$1/4$ yard each of 5 shaded fabrics
Number of blocks	36	$1/2$ yard of the 6th (lightest) shade
Block size	6" finished	1 $1/4$ yards background fabric
Log width	1" finished	1 $1/2$ yards border fabric
Number of rounds	6	2 yards backing fabric
Border	1" inner border,	$1/2$ yard binding fabric
	6" outer border	

Cutting instructions

Strip piece the "center" and the first log. Make 1 $1/2$ strip units from 1 $1/2$ selvage-to-selvage cuts of fabric A (the darkest fabric) and background fabric. See page 19. Make 36 crosscuts each 1 $1/2$" wide.

Shaded logs: Cut 36 sets from the fabrics listed.

		Background logs: Cut 36 sets.	
1 $1/2$" x 2 $1/2$"	fabric B	1 $1/2$" x 2 $1/2$"	
1 $1/2$" x 3 $1/2$"	fabric C	1 $1/2$" x 3 $1/2$"	
1 $1/2$" x 4 $1/2$"	fabric D	1 $1/2$" x 4 $1/2$"	
1 $1/2$" x 5 $1/2$"	fabric E	1 $1/2$" x 5 $1/2$"	
1 $1/2$" x 6 $1/2$"	fabric F (lightest)		

Inner border: From background fabric, cut 2 strips 1 $1/2$" x 36 $1/2$" and 2 strips 1 $1/2$" x 38 $1/2$".
Outer border: Cut 2 strips 6 $1/2$" x 38 $1/2$" and 2 strips 6 $1/2$" x 50 $1/2$", parallel to the selvages.

Spring Flowers (page 74)

This is the simplest possible version of the Cabin Rose block. The octagonal set is striking and very easy to do.

		Fabric required
Quilt size	33" x 33"	
Number of blocks	13	$^{1}/_{8}$ yard fabric for "centers" (flowers)
Block size	4" finished	$^{1}/_{4}$ yard green fabric
Log width	1" finished	$^{1}/_{2}$ yard background fabric (includes finishing triangles)
Number of rounds	2	$^{1}/_{4}$ yard inner border fabric
Border	$^{1}/_{2}$" inner border,	1 $^{1}/_{4}$ yards border fabric (includes binding)
	4" outer border	

Cutting instructions

Centers: Speed piece the centers and the first logs. Make a selvage-to-selvage cut of flower fabric 2 $^{1}/_{2}$" wide, and a similar cut of background fabric 1 $^{1}/_{2}$" wide. Seam the two together and press the seam allowances toward the background fabric. Make 13 crosscuts 2 $^{1}/_{2}$" wide.

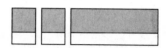

Stem log: Speed piece the stem logs. Cut a piece of background fabric 2 $^{1}/_{2}$" x 24". Cut a piece of green fabric 1 $^{1}/_{2}$" x 24". Seam together and press the seam allowances toward the background fabric. Make 13 crosscuts 1 $^{1}/_{2}$" wide.

Leaf logs: Cut 13 sets from the green fabric.

   1 $^{1}/_{2}$" x 3 $^{1}/_{2}$"
   1 $^{1}/_{2}$" x 4 $^{1}/_{2}$"

Follow the piecing diagram.

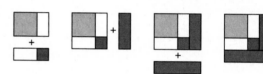

NOTE: See page 150 for diagonal set illustrations. Use the measurements below for the sashing strips and finishing triangles.

Sashing strips: Cut the following from background fabric.

18	1 $^{1}/_{2}$" x 4 $^{1}/_{2}$"
2	1 $^{1}/_{2}$" x 6 $^{1}/_{2}$"
2	1 $^{1}/_{2}$" x 26 $^{1}/_{2}$"
2	1 $^{1}/_{2}$" x 16 $^{1}/_{2}$"

Sew the short strips to the blocks, then assemble the blocks into diagonal rows.

Edge triangles: From background fabric, cut 4 squares 4 $^{7}/_{8}$" x 4 $^{7}/_{8}$". Cut each in half diagonally to make 8 triangles. (Do not cut the corner triangles yet.) Sew the triangles to the ends of the diagonal rows. Sew the rows together, with sashing strips between each row as illustrated on page 150.

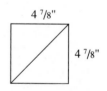

Trim to even up the edges before adding the border. I trimmed a little away from the top and bottom and sides at this point, but not from the four diagonal edges at the corners.

Inner border: Make 3 cuts each 1" wide from the inner border fabric. Sew the inner border to all 8 sides of the quilt. Do the four long edges first, press, and then the four diagonal corners. Trim off the ends of the strips. As you sew the strips on, be careful not to stretch the bias edges of the triangles.

Now add the four corner triangles that square up the quilt. Cut a square from the *border* fabric, 7 $^{1}/_{2}$" x 7 $^{1}/_{2}$", and cut in half diagonally twice to make 4 triangles. Sew these to the 4 corners. Trim away the excess.

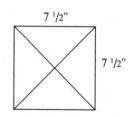

Outer border: From the border fabric, make 4 selvage-to-selvage cuts 4 $^{1}/_{2}$" wide. Sew to the edges of the quilt and miter the corners (see page 151).

Cabin Rose (page 76)

I have a special fondness for this quilt because it was the real beginning of my career as a quilting teacher and author. I started by teaching introductory quiltmaking once or twice on the island where I live, and then when I showed this quilt to the owners of a quilt shop on the mainland nearby, they asked me to teach it in a class. The rest, as they say, is history.

Like the simpler version Spring Flowers, the quilt is very simple to piece but is a real charmer. Because the design is so angular and I think flowers should be graceful, I hand quilted both quilts in flowing lines (see page 147).

		Fabric required
Quilt size	41" x 41"	scraps of pink fabrics, or $^1/_4$ yard total
Number of blocks	13	scraps of green fabrics, or $^1/_2$ yard total
Block size	6" finished	1 yard background fabric
Log width	1" finished	$^1/_4$ yard inner border fabric
Number of rounds	4	1 yard outer border fabric
Border	$^1/_2$" inner border,	1 $^1/_2$ yards backing fabric
	5" outer border	$^1/_2$ yard binding fabric

Cutting instructions
Flowers: From a variety of pinks, cut 13 sets.

 2 $^1/_2$" x 2 $^1/_2$"
 1 $^1/_2$" x 2 $^1/_2$"
 1 $^1/_2$" x 3 $^1/_2$"

Background logs: From the background fabric, cut 13 pieces 1 $^1/_2$" x 3 $^1/_2$".
Stem logs: Cut 13 green squares 1 $^1/_2$" x 1 $^1/_2$" and 13 background logs 1 $^1/_2$" x 3 $^1/_2$", and seam them together. Press the seam allowances toward the background fabric.
Leaf logs: Cut 13 sets from a variety of green fabrics.

 1 $^1/_2$" x 4 $^1/_2$"
 1 $^1/_2$" x 5 $^1/_2$"
 1 $^1/_2$" x 5 $^1/_2$"
 1 $^1/_2$" x 6 $^1/_2$"

NOTE: See page 150 for diagonal set directions. Use the measurements below for sashing strips and finishing triangles.

Sashing strips: Cut the following from background fabric.

 18   1 $^1/_2$" x 6 $^1/_2$"
  2   1 $^1/_2$" x 8 $^1/_2$"
  2   1 $^1/_2$" x 36 $^1/_2$"
  2   1 $^1/_2$" x 22 $^1/_2$"

Edge triangles: Cut 4 squares 6 $^7/_8$" x 6 $^7/_8$" and cut in half diagonally to make 8 edge triangles. Assemble blocks, edge triangles, and sashing strips as described for Spring Flowers. Trim the four sides (but not the four diagonal corners) to $^1/_4$" away from the corners of the leaves. In the quilt Spring Flowers, I trimmed away less and added the inner border at this point. In this quilt, I trimmed away more and added a strip of background fabric to the sides and top and bottom, to stabilize the bias edges of the triangles before adding the inner border. Cut 4 strips of background fabric 1 $^1/_2$" x 30" and sew to the four sides of the quilt. Pin each side on a flat surface before you sew, and be careful not to stretch the bias edges. Trim the ends.

Inner border and corner triangles: Make 4 cuts of the inner border fabric each 1" wide. Sew a strip to each of the four sides, press and trim, then sew the left-over strips to the four diagonal corners. Now add the four corner triangles that square up the quilt. Cut a square from the *border* fabric, 9 $^1/_2$" x 9 $^1/_2$", and cut in half diagonally twice to make 4 triangles. Sew these to the four corners. Trim away the excess.

Outer border: From the border fabric, make 4 selvage-to-selvage cuts 5 $^1/_2$" wide. Sew to the edges of the quilt and miter the corners (see page 151). Since the quilt finishes at 41" square, unless your border fabric is a healthy 44" wide you may want to make the border a little narrower.

Each tree is an off-center log cabin block with a large "center" and eight logs. Six of the eight logs are speed-pieced, and the "center" itself is also pieced. The blocks are set together on point. The border strips are added side by side in a spiral, as if the tree section were the center of a large log cabin block.

The blocks can be assembled quickly if you speed piece, which you can do if each tree is identical. Because a different green fabric is used here for each log, the quilt still looks quite scrappy. If you make a large quilt with more than 25 or so trees, you will need more than one strip unit for each log and can vary the fabrics so that your trees are not all alike. You can use one background fabric or mix a variety of white-on-muslin prints, as was done here; using a variety enhances the snowfall look of the background.

The trunks could be appliqued onto 4" (finished) squares of background, but I chose to piece them instead.

Quilt size	30" x 40"
Number of blocks	8
Block size	8" finished
Log width	1" finished
Number of rounds	4
Border	3 strips 1" wide added to each side

Fabric required
$^1/_8$ yard each of 3 green prints, and $^1/_4$ yard each of
    5 prints, or scraps (includes border)
scraps of brown prints
scraps of white-on-muslin prints
$^1/_2$ yard white-on-muslin print for edge triangles and
    top border
1 yard backing fabric
$^1/_2$ yard binding fabric

Cutting and assembly instructions:
NOTE: reserve the $^1/_2$ yard of one muslin print for the edge triangles and top border strip.

CENTERS
    Cut 4 squares 5" x 5" from a variety of muslins. Cut the squares in half diagonally to make 8 triangles.
    Cut 8 squares 3 $^1/_2$" x 3 $^1/_2$" from a variety of muslins. Cut the squares in half diagonally to make 16 triangles.
    Cut 8 pieces 1 $^1/_2$" x 3 $^1/_2$" from a variety of brown prints.

Mixing the small muslin triangles, sew one to each long edge of the tree trunks. Match the edges at the bottom of the trunks, as shown; the top edges will not match. Press seam allowances toward the trunks.

Sew each trunk section to a large triangle. Press seam allowances toward the large triangle. Trim each piece to 4 $^1/_2$" x 4 $^1/_2$".

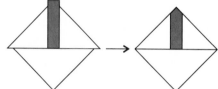

LOGS
Before you cut any logs, decide the position in the block of each of your green and muslin fabrics. Starting with the first log added to the trunk square, the logs are numbered 1 through 8.

The first two logs are not speed-pieced. Cut 13 sets.
    log 1   1 $^1/_2$" x 4 $^1/_2$"
    log 2   1 $^1/_2$" x 5 $^1/_2$"

The other six logs are speed-pieced, each from a piece of green and a piece of muslin.

	green	muslin
log 3	13" x 4 $^1/_2$"	13" x 1 $^1/_2$"
log 4	13" x 5 $^1/_2$"	13" x 1 $^1/_2$"
log 5	13" x 3 $^1/_2$"	13" x 3 $^1/_2$"
log 6	13" x 4 $^1/_2$"	13" x 3 $^1/_2$"
log 7	13" x 2 $^1/_2$"	13" x 5 $^1/_2$"
log 8	13" x 3 $^1/_2$"	13" x 5 $^1/_2$"

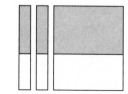

Sew each green piece to its corresponding muslin piece. Press all seam allowances toward the green. Make 8 crosscuts each 1 $^1/_2$" wide from each strip unit.

Edge triangles: From the ¹/₂ yard of muslin cut 3 squares 8 ⁷/₈" x 8 ⁷/₈". Cut the squares in half diagonally to make 6 triangles.

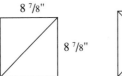

Corner triangles: From the same muslin, cut a square 9 ¹/₄" x 9 ¹/₄". Cut it in half diagonally twice to make 4 corner triangles.

Lay out the blocks and triangles as shown and sew each row together and press, then sew the rows together and press. If necessary, trim.

Cut a strip of the same muslin 2 ¹/₂" x 34 ¹/₂". Sew the strip to the top of the quilt.

Border: The border is made of 12 green strips. Decide the position of each fabric before you cut. Start with strip 1 at the top edge and add the strips either clockwise or counterclockwise, pressing seam allowances toward the strip just added before sewing on the next strip.

1	1 ¹/₂" x 34 ¹/₂"
2	1 ¹/₂" x 25 ¹/₂"
3	1 ¹/₂" x 35 ¹/₂"
4	1 ¹/₂" x 26 ¹/₂"
5	1 ¹/₂" x 36 ¹/₂"
6	1 ¹/₂" x 27 ¹/₂"
7	1 ¹/₂" x 37 ¹/₂"
8	1 ¹/₂" x 28 ¹/₂"
9	1 ¹/₂" x 38 ¹/₂"
10	1 ¹/₂" x 29 ¹/₂"
11	1 ¹/₂" x 39 ¹/₂"
12	1 ¹/₂" x 30 ¹/₂"

Quilting
The pieced trees were quilted in the ditch, and the border in a sawtooth design. Trees were quilted freehand in the background triangles in the lower edge and corners, and irregular five-pointed stars were quilted in the upper background triangles. Use short pieces of ¹/₄" masking tape to outline the star shapes.

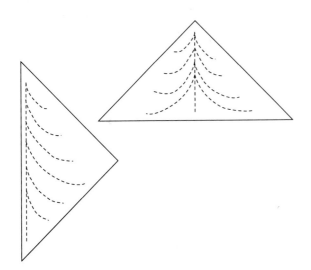

Draw irregular stars with short lengths of ¹/₄" masking tape and quilt around them.

57

Purple Mums (page 74; diagram on page 48)

This is the Cabin Rose block in a more formal setting. The flower blocks themselves are very controlled, and the extra-wide border adds elegance.

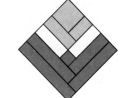

		Fabric required:
Quilt size	33" x 33"	$^1/_8$ yard each of 2 flower fabrics and 3 greens
Number of blocks	5	1 yard background fabric (includes binding)
Block size	6" finished	$^1/_8$ yard inner border fabric
Log width	1" finished	1 yard outer border fabric
Number of rounds	4	1 $^1/_4$ yards backing fabric
Border	$^1/_2$" inner border, 7" outer border	

Cutting instructions

Prepare five blocks, following the instructions for Cabin Rose. Use one fabric for each pair of logs; refer to color photograph.

Sashing strips: Cut the following from background fabric.

6 $^7/_8$"

6 $^7/_8$"

    8   1 $^1/_2$" x 6 $^1/_2$"
    2   1 $^1/_2$" x 8 $^1/_2$"
    2   1 $^1/_2$" x 22 $^1/_2$"

Edge triangles: Cut 2 squares 6 $^7/_8$" x 6 $^7/_8$" and cut in half diagonally to make 4 edge triangles.

Assemble blocks, edge triangles, and sashing strips as described above for Spring Flowers. Trim the four sides (but not the four diagonal corners) to $^1/_4$" away from the corners of the leaves.

Cut 4 strips of background fabric 1 $^1/_2$" x 12" and sew to the four sides of the quilt. Pin each side on a flat surface before you sew, and be careful not to stretch the bias edge. Trim the ends.

Inner border and corner triangles: See Cabin Rose.
Outer border: From the border fabric, make 3 selvage-to-selvage cuts 7 $^1/_2$" wide and one cut 6 $^1/_2$" wide, for the top border. Sew to the edges of the quilt and miter the corners (see page 151).

Watercolor (page 72)

This is a good design to emphasize a linear print. I used both clockwise and counterclockwise piecing, so that in each round of the Barn Raising all of the logs of the watercolor fabric run in only one direction. The wide border provides a good view of the beautiful and unusual fabric.

		Fabric required
Quilt size	43" x 43"	2 $^1/_2$ yards linear print (includes
Number of blocks	36	border and binding)
Block size	5" finished	$^1/_3$ yard each of three accent fabrics
Log width	1 $^1/_4$" finished	1 $^1/_2$ yards backing fabric
Number of rounds	3	
Border	1 $^1/_4$" inner border, 5" outer border	

Cutting instructions

NOTE: If you are using a linear print, cut the strips for the centers first, then the outer border pieces, then cut the logs and binding strips from the remainder.
Fabric A is the innermost accent color, fabric B the middle accent, and fabric C the outer accent color and inner border.

Centers: Speed piece all of the "centers" and first logs. Cut strips 1 $^3/_4$" wide: 24" of fabric A, 40" of fabric B, and 9" of fabric C. Cut matching lengths of the linear print, with the linear design running *across* each strip. Make 1 $^3/_4$" crosscuts, 12 of fabric A, 20 of fabric B, and 4 of fabric C.

Linear print logs: Cut 36 sets, with linear design running the length of each log. The first log (the "center") has already been speed pieced.

    1 $^3/_4$" x 3"
    1 $^3/_4$" x 4 $^1/_4$"
    1 $^3/_4$" x 5 $^1/_2$"

Accent logs: Cut 12 sets of fabric A, 20 sets of fabric B, and 4 sets of fabric C. The first log has already been speed pieced.

    1 $^3/_4$" x 3"
    1 $^3/_4$" x 4 $^1/_4$"

Rainbow Lightning *by Mary Perillo, Seattle, Washington, 1984-1987, 76" x 96". The black prints used for the dark half of each log cabin block intensify the other colors. Hand quilted. Instructions on page 25.*

*Detail, **Peter's Quilt** by Mary Ellen Walker, Vashon Island, Washington, 1990, 92" x 107". A traditional Barn-Raising design in solid colors and a few subtle prints. The red squares seem to dance across the surface of the quilt because they are not the centers of the blocks, but the first logs. Hand quilted. Instructions on page 23.*

***Say When**, 1992, 36" x 36". When you make a log cabin block with 15 $^1/_2$ rounds, one block is enough for a quilt! The shaded range of 16 red fabrics runs light to dark in one half of the block, and dark to light in the other half. Hand quilted. Instructions on page 26.*

Sawtooth Star, 1989, 42" x 42". Instructions on page 24.

Toys, 1989, 44" x 44". The traditional Barn-Raising design, with large centers cut from a pretty motif fabric. Each block was hand quilted in a different design. Instructions on page 23; quilting diagrams on page 144.

61

Friends in the Forest *by Corki Duncan, Snohomish, Washington, 1990, 67" x 84". Corki surrounded signed Schoolhouse friendship blocks with log cabin blocks, and then designed a speed-pieced border of pine trees against a starry night sky. Hand quilted by Beth Payne. Instructions on page 27.*

Don and Rachel's Quilt, *1989, 66" x 66". This quilt is proof positive that you can start a wedding quilt a week before the wedding and finish it on time. It was assembled by the machine quilt-as-you-go technique, and finished off with a speed-pieced border. Instructions on page 28.*

Back, **Don and Rachel's Quilt.** *The backing squares of this quilt-as-you-go project were cut from several blue prints. The blocks were arranged so the squares make a symmetrical design on the back. The blue strip across the top is a sleeve for hanging the quilt.*

Old-Fashioned Roses, *1990, 42" x 49". The traditional Straight-Furrows design, in three colors rather than two. Hand quilted. Instructions on page 25.*

Sophisticated Lady, *1992, 46" x 46". An elegant quilt top pieced from just two fabrics. Large centers break up the stark lines of the Barn-Raising design. Instructions on page 24.*

Deep Purple Dreams, *1992, 50"*
x 50". Although it appears
complex, the design is made of
just two different log cabin
blocks in a four-block repeat.
Instructions on page 29.

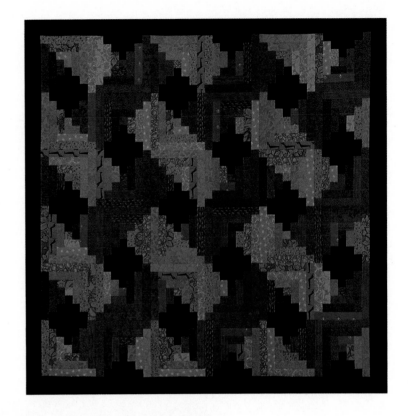

Big City Blues, *1991, 50" x 56".*
This is acutally a traditional Streak
o' Lightning design, made with
rectangular blocks. Instructions on
page 37.

Persia, *1991, 48" x 66". The elongated design and richly detailed contemporary fabrics contribute to a Middle Eastern look. Instructions on page 37.*

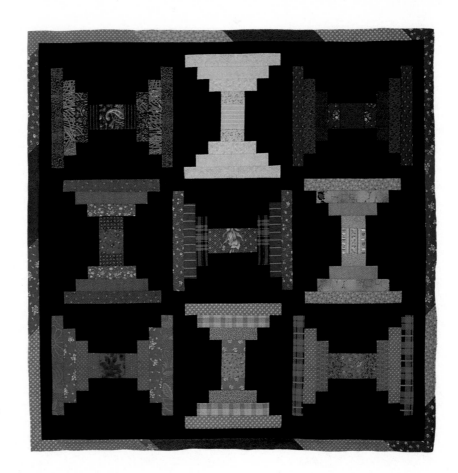

Scrappy Spools, 1989, 42" x 42". *Bright primary colors against black make a vivid wall quilt. Assembled by the machine quilt-as-you-go technique. Instructions on page 42.*

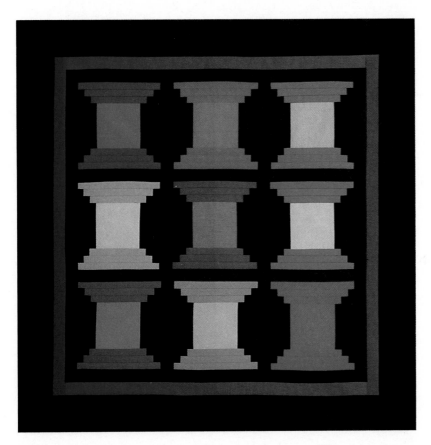

Amish Spools by *Virginia Morrison, Seattle, Washington, 1991, 32" x 32". Small Courthouse Steps blocks (the logs are only $^1/_2$" finished) in Amish solids. Instructions on page 43.*

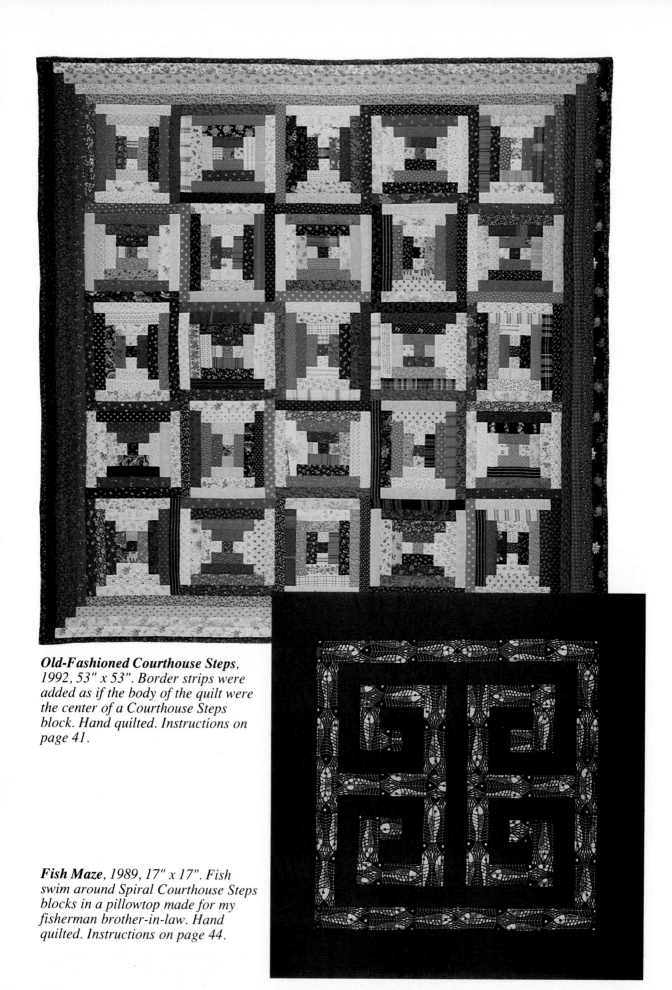

Old-Fashioned Courthouse Steps, 1992, 53" x 53". Border strips were added as if the body of the quilt were the center of a Courthouse Steps block. Hand quilted. Instructions on page 41.

Fish Maze, 1989, 17" x 17". Fish swim around Spiral Courthouse Steps blocks in a pillowtop made for my fisherman brother-in-law. Hand quilted. Instructions on page 44.

Shaded Placemats, 1992, 13" x 18". Seven fabrics in a shaded series are assembled machine quilt-as-you-go into rectangular Courthouse Steps blocks, one for each placemat. Instructions on page 41.

Courthouse Stars by Karen Gabriel, Princeton Junction, New Jersey, 1991, 62" x 62". Only 16 Courthouse Steps blocks are needed to make this lap-size quilt. Instructions on page 44.

Spiral Placemats, 1992, 13" x 19". The machine quilt-as-you-go technique makes these placemats a quick project. Instructions on page 47.

Yellow Spools by Lorraine Herge, Concord, North Carolina, and Janet Kime, 1991, 71" x 71". Sashing strips separate Courthouse Steps blocks that imitate spools of thread. The striking border is a combination of log cabin and Courthouse Steps blocks. Instructions on page 42.

Under the Sea by Joan Hanson, Seattle, Washington, 1991, 40" x 56". Joan made Spiral Courthouse Steps blocks from hand-dyed sea green fabrics for her underwater fantasy. Instructions on page 45.

Watercolor, 1991, 43" x 43".
Off-center log cabin blocks
emphasize the linear
watercolor print and make
this a subtly different Barn
Raising. Hand quilted.
Instructions on page 58.

Sparkle Plenty by Joel T. Patz,
Seattle, Washington, 1991, 44"
x 44". Inspired by a quilt by
Sharyn Craig, this vivid wall
hanging is machine stipple-
quilted with metallic thread.
Instructions on page 91.

Stars and Spirals by Susan Konecki, Vashon Island, Washington, 1991, 27" x 26". Spiral Courthouse Steps blocks make a vivid setting for scrappy sawtooth star blocks. Instructions on page 45.

Rhapsody in Blue by Marie Blichfeldt, Vashon Island, Washington, 1989, 40" x 40". Unlike most log cabin variations, off-center log cabins are often set on point. Hand quilted. Instructions on page 53.

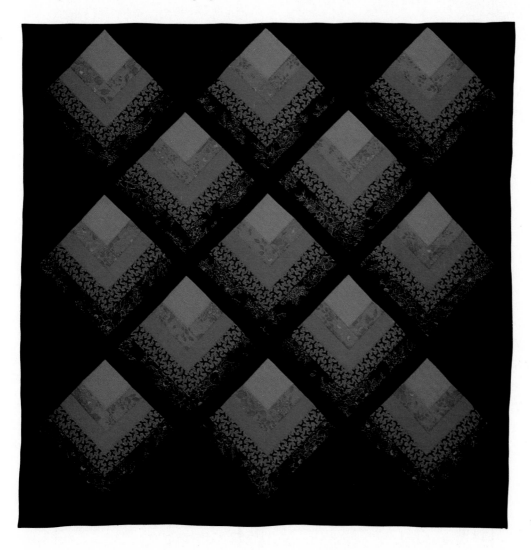

73

Spring Flowers, 1989, 33" x 33". Simple off-center log cabin blocks, bright colors, and an interesting set make a sprightly wall hanging. Hand quilted. Instructions on page 54.

Purple Mums, 1989, 33" x 33". The striking border fabric is featured in this wall hanging; the pieced center is small and precise. Hand quilted. Instructions on page 58.

Green Pinwheels, 1991, 50"
x 50". A carefully shaded
series of green fabrics adds
depth to this design.
Instructions on page 53.

Pine Trees by Carol Kime, Battle Creek, Michigan, 1991, 30" x 40".
Hand quilted by the author. Instructions on page 56.

Cabin Rose, 1989, 41" x 41".
Scrappy off-center log cabin
blocks are set on point and
separated by sashing strips.
Hand quilted. Instructions on
page 55.

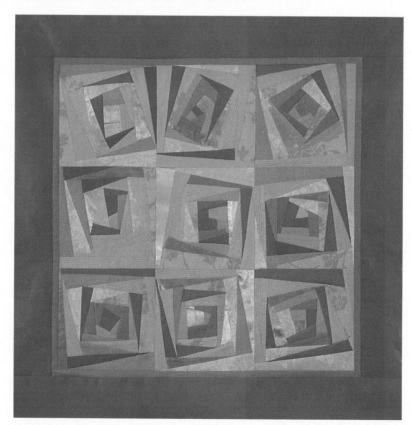

Fractured Ice, 1992, 30" x 30".
Spikes of satins and silky
polyesters glitter and flash in this
very irregular log cabin.
Instructions on page 95.

Goofus, 1991, 30" x 36". Strips and scraps, just for fun. Instructions on page 95.

Irregular Placemats, 1992, 13" x 19".
*Each placemat is a different
arrangement of six irregular log
cabin blocks. Machine quilted.
Instructions on page 95.*

Mary's Chimneys and Cornerstones by Mary Hales, Camano Island, Washington, 1990, 51" x 51". Machine quilted by Patsi Hanseth. Instructions on page 101.

Frances's Chimneys and Cornerstones by Frances McCadden, Lynnwood, Washington, 1990, 43" x 43". Instructions on page 101.

Rectangular Chimneys and Cornerstones by Joel T. Patz, Seattle, Washington, 1990, 58" x 76". A rectangular version of Chimneys and Cornerstones in the Barn-Raising design. Instructions on page 104.

The Gerbil Quilt, 1989, 48" x 48". Chimneys and Cornerstones in the traditional Light-and-Dark design. The colors remind me of my office gerbils, Cagney and Lacey. Instructions on page 102.

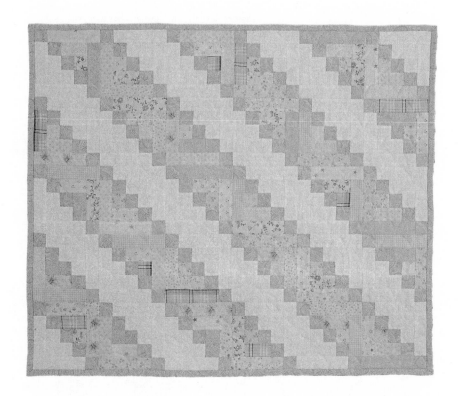

Yellow Chimneys and Cornerstones, 1990, 37" x 31". Hand quilted. Instructions on page 102.

Cornered V's, 1991, 40" x 54". Cornerstones are not always dark or solid colors; here a large-scale floral print is used for both the border and the cornerstones. Machine quilted. Instructions on page 103.

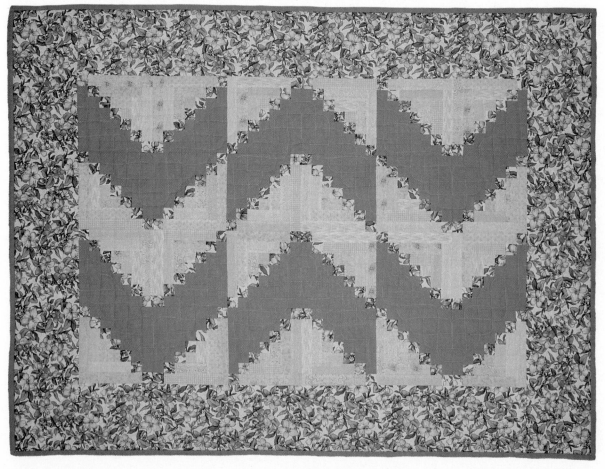

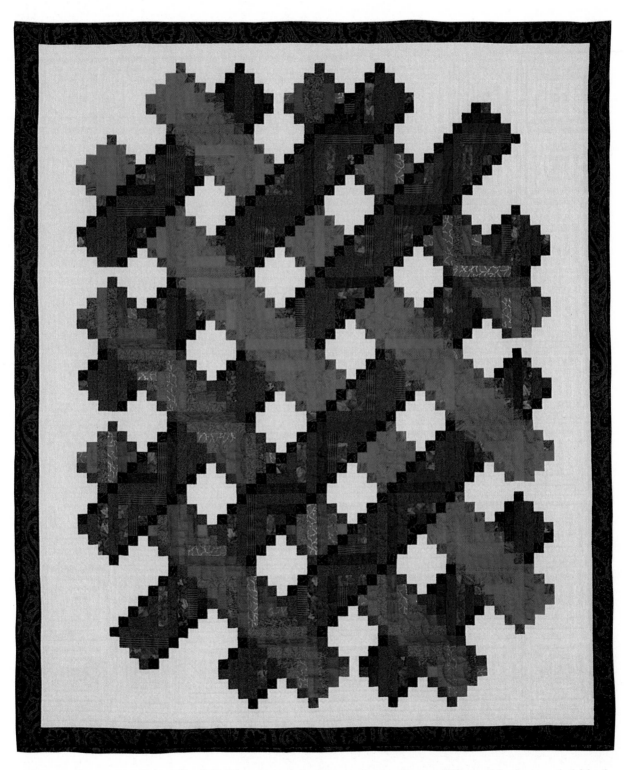

Vashon Interweave, *1991, 60" x 76". The central design employs only two different blocks in a 4x4 block repeat; the edge blocks, on the other hand, are pretty exotic. Hand quilted. Instructions on page 107.*

***Bigger and Better** by Karen Sheard, Los Angeles, California, 1991, 80" x 103". Karen used a rather wild pink fabric for both the cornerstones and two of the light logs in each block, creating an interesting secondary design. Instructions on page 102.*

***Pinks and Purples**, 1992, 51" x 59". There is no limit to the number of designs possible with the gently curved lines of Thick-and-Thin blocks. Instructions on page 115.*

Log Cabin Variation by Vivian Heiner, Seattle, Washington, 1990, 43" x 43". Another traditional Light-and-Dark design, this time scrappy with bright red centers. Machine quilted. Instructions on page 115.

Crocus, 1989, 42" x 42". Joyce Schlotzhauer curved two-patch system books are good sources for design ideas for Thick-and-Thin log cabins. Hand quilted. Instructions on page 116.

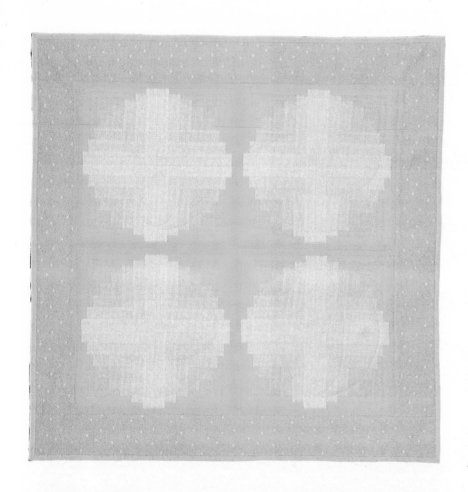

Four Suns, 1992, 38" x 38". Thick-and-Thin blocks made from a series of hand-dyed fabrics, in the traditional Light-and-Dark design. Machine quilted. Instructions on page 113.

Christmas Wreath by Mary Perillo, Seattle, Washington, 1990, 42" x 42". Hand quilted with gold metallic thread, including the caption "Peace on Earth" across the bottom border. Instructions on page 113.

Scarlet Ribbons, 1990, 28" x
28". A variation of Straight
Furrows, in a tight range of ten
red fabrics. Hand quilted.
Instructions on page 114.

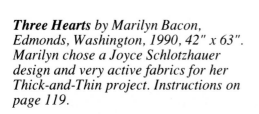

Three Hearts by Marilyn Bacon,
Edmonds, Washington, 1990, 42" x 63".
Marilyn chose a Joyce Schlotzhauer
design and very active fabrics for her
Thick-and-Thin project. Instructions on
page 119.

Christmas Tree #1, 1991, 50" x 70". Rectangular blocks make this tree more graceful than Christmas trees made from square log cabin blocks. Instructions on page 135.

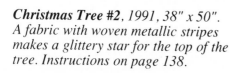

Christmas Tree #2, 1991, 38" x 50". A fabric with woven metallic stripes makes a glittery star for the top of the tree. Instructions on page 138.

Stars and Stripes *by June Williams, Seattle, Washington, 1991, 41" x 41". June quilted this patriotic wall hanging during the war with Iraq. The three yellow ribbons were added in recognition of the three members of her family who were stationed in Saudi Arabia. All returned home safely. Machine quilted. Instructions on page 133.*

Old Glory, *1990, 44" x 35". The distortion in the lines of Straight Furrows, which occurs to some extent in every Cabin Stars design, makes this quilt look like a flag rippling in the breeze. Hand quilted. Instructions on page 132.*

Pastel Cabin Stars, *1990, 39" x 39".*
Instructions on page 131.

Star Wheels *by Jordan Riley, Gig Harbor, Washington, 1991, 72" x 72". The omission of the partial stars on the outer edge of the quilt and the two types of log cabin blocks make this a complicated quilt to plan and execute, but the effect is lovely and well worth the effort. Instructions on page 135.*

Dark Stars, 1990, 67" x
67". Hand quilted.
Instructions on page 134.

Straight Furrows by Margaret Brevig, Tacoma, Washington,
1991, 66" x 55". Instructions on page 131.

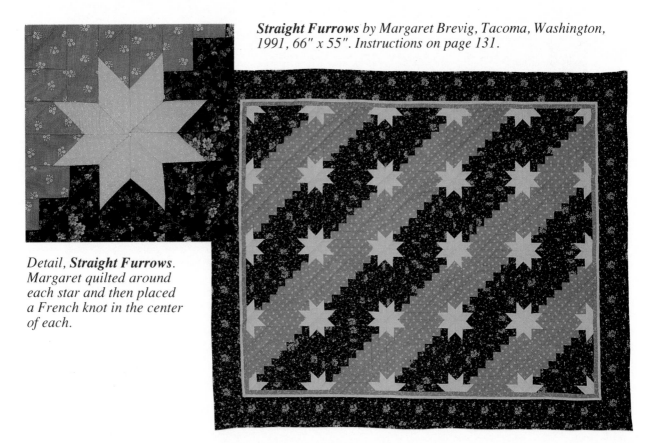

Detail, **Straight Furrows**.
*Margaret quilted around
each star and then placed
a French knot in the center
of each.*

Waiting for Ric *by Ginny Hoffman, Southworth, Washington, 1991, 84" x 106". Ginny started this quilt in a class held in January, 1991, during the war with Iraq. She made the quilt for her son Ric, who was stationed in Saudi Arabia. She was worried about him, of course, and the quilt was a way to do something positive for him while he was in danger so far away. As she listened to the news on CNN every day, she pieced Ric's quilt. He came home safely that July. Instructions on page 133.*

Piece 12 blocks with fabric A, 20 with fabric B, and 4 with fabric C. Piece half of each color group as mirror images of the other half.

Inner border: From fabric C cut 2 strips 1 ³/₄" x 30 ¹/₂" and 2 strips 1 ³/₄" x 33".

Outer border: From the linear print with the design running lengthwise, cut 2 strips 5 ¹/₂" x 33" and 2 strips 5 ¹/₂" x 43".

Sparkle Plenty (page 72)

Quilt size	44" x 44"
Number of blocks	36
Block size	6 ¹/₄" finished
Log width	1 ¹/₄" finished
Number of rounds	4
Border	¹/₄" inner accent; 3 ¹/₄" pieced

Fabric required

2 yards assorted tropical prints
2 ¹/₂ yards black (includes border and binding)
¹/₄ yard inner border accent fabric
2 ¹/₂ yards backing fabric

Cutting instructions

Black logs: Cut 36 sets.
  1 ³/₄" x 3"
  1 ³/₄" x 4 ¹/₄"
  1 ³/₄" x 5 ¹/₂"

Print logs: Cut 36 sets from a variety of fabrics.
  1 ³/₄" x 3"
  1 ³/₄" x 4 ¹/₄"
  1 ³/₄" x 5 ¹/₂"
  1 ³/₄" x 6 ³/₄"

Inner accent border: Cut 2 strips ¹/₂" x 38" and 2 strips ¹/₂" x 38 ¹/₂".

Pieced border: Make 12 selvage-to-selvage cuts 1" wide from a variety of fabrics, and 12 selvage-to-selvage cuts 1" wide from black. Assemble 4 strip units A and 4 strip units B, pressing all seam allowances toward the print fabrics. Make 160 crosscuts 1" wide from the A strip units, and 156 from the B strip units.

A

B

Alternating A and B crosscuts, sew together 76 crosscuts for each of the 4 borders. Press all seam allowances in one direction.

From the black fabric, cut 4 strips 1 ¹/₄" x 38 ¹/₂" for the inner borders and 4 strips 1 ¹/₂" x 38 ¹/₂" for the outer borders. Sew to the inside and outside edges of each pieced border strip. Press seam allowances toward the black strips.

For the corner blocks, piece 4 nine-patch blocks from the remaining A and B crosscuts. Cut 4 sets of each measurement listed from black, and follow the piecing diagram to add a border around each little block. Piece two corner blocks as shown and two mirror images (that is, reverse pieces 3 and 4).

  1   1 ¹/₄" x 2"
  2   1 ¹/₂" x 2"
  3   1 ¹/₄" x 3 ³/₄"
  4   1 ¹/₂" x 3 ³/₄"

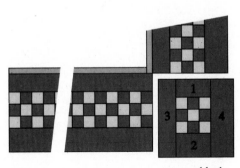

corner block

Sew two of the pieced borders to two opposite sides of the quilt. Sew the corner blocks to the ends of the remaining two pieced borders, and add the border strips to the quilt. Be careful to place the corner blocks so that the wider borders (pieces 2 and 4) are on the outside edge.

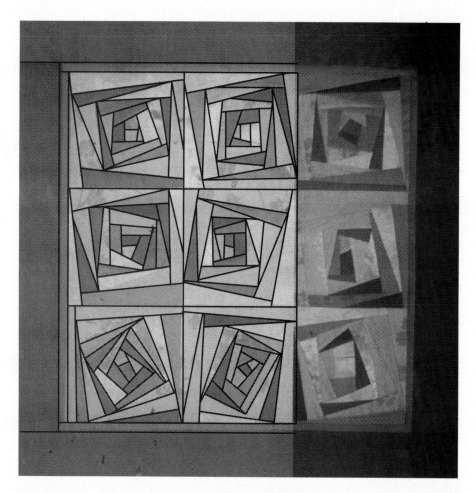

Fractured Ice*; color plate on page 77, instructions on page 95.*

Irregular Log Cabins

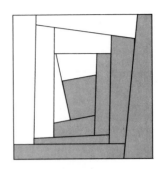

Irregular log cabins are just like traditional log cabins, except that the logs are made from fabric scraps of random shapes and sizes. The block is then trimmed into a square.

Irregular log cabin blocks can be used for any of the traditional designs. Depending on the fabrics used and the angles, the result can be as jagged and jumpy as the Barn Raising below, or as sophisticated as Fractured Ice (page 76), or as whimsical as Goofus (page 77).

To piece an irregular log cabin, gather up all the little scraps of fabric you couldn't bear to throw away, all the left-over strips from speed-piecing projects, the ends trimmed from mitered borders, even the waste strips from clean-up cuts. Anything at least 1" wide is usable.

Start with a center square about 1 ½" x 1 ½". I often start with a piece that isn't square. It is surprising how difficult it is to purposefully make a block with lots of odd angles, and if you start with a lopsided center you will have oddnesses right off the bat.

Right sides together, seam the center to another scrap. This is a good time to use the speed-piecing technique described on page 16, since you aren't precutting your logs.

Cut the pieces apart and trim any messiness away from the seam allowances before pressing. As you add logs, add some at angles. Make some logs skinny and some wide. As always, press seam allowances toward the log just added.

press →

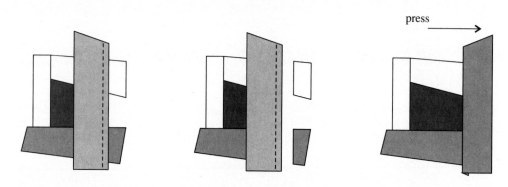

When your log has reached the size you want, trim it to a square. I trimmed the blocks for Goofus 6" square (5 ½" finished), so I could use my 6" square acrylic ruler. If you use a clear ruler to trim the blocks, you can see the block through the ruler and decide where to trim. Whatever size you decide upon, cut a square of template plastic or cardboard that size and keep it at your sewing machine. Check your block as you add the last round and select scraps that will bring your block up to the correct size.

If you plan to use your blocks in a traditional log cabin design, the quilt will look better if all the blocks end on the same side, with either a pair of dark logs or a pair of light logs but not a mixture. The blocks do not all have to have the same number of rounds, but the same half of the block (light or dark) should always be larger. Otherwise, there may be so much distortion that the lines of the design will be obscured.

Instructions: Irregular Log Cabins

Goofus (page 77)

Quilt size	30" x 36"
Number of blocks	30
Block size	5 ¹/₂" finished
Log width	varies, ¹/₂"-2" finished
Number of rounds	3
Border	irregular

Fabric required
about 2 yards total scraps,
   including border
1 yard backing fabric
¹/₂ yard binding fabric

Cutting instructions
Borders: Cut border strips from a variety of fabrics in a variety of widths. Add one strip at a time, proceeding counterclockwise around the quilt, as if the design were the center of a log cabin block.

Irregular Placemats (page 77)

Quilt size	13" x 19"
Number of blocks	6 per placemat
Block size	6" finished
Log width	varies, ¹/₂"-2" finished
Number of rounds	3

Fabric required
about ¹/₂ yard total for each
   placemat
¹/₂ yard each of four fabrics, or
   1 ¹/₄ yard of one fabric for
   backing and binding
1 yard Pellon®

Finishing instructions
After each placemat top has been assembled, cut 4 pieces of backing each 14 ¹/₂" x 20". Cut 4 pieces of Pellon® the same size. Sandwich the backing, batting, and top. Mark the quilting lines with chalk and a ruler, then pin the layers together with straight pins every 2" along the chalk lines. Trim away excess batting and backing ¹/₄" beyond the raw edge of the placemat top. Machine quilt, starting and stopping at the edges and backstitching at each end. Bind the edges (see page 153).

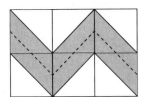 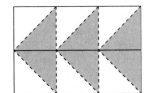  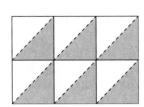

Fractured Ice (page 76; diagram on page 92)

The blocks of this quilt are irregular log cabins taken a step further: many logs are crossed by the next log at such a steep angle that one end of the log is narrowed to a point, resulting in wedges instead of logs.

Quilt size	30" x 30"
Number of blocks	9
Block size	7 ¹/₂" finished
Log width	varies, up to 2" finished
Border	¹/₂" inner border,
	3" outer border

Fabric required
2 yards total of a variety of cottons and polyester
   fabrics, including satins
¹/₂ yard outer border fabric
1 yard backing fabric
¹/₂ yard binding fabric

Cutting instructions
Inner border: Cut 2 strips 1" x 23" and 2 strips 1" x 24".
Outer border: Cut 2 strips 3 ¹/₂" x 24" and 2 strips 3 ¹/₂" x 30".

The Gerbil Quilt; *color plate on page 79, instructions on page 102.*

Chimneys and Cornerstones

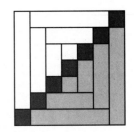

Chimneys and Cornerstones is a simple log cabin variation in which the line between the dark and light halves of the block is accented with a row of squares (the "cornerstones"). Notice that the Chimneys and Cornerstone block is divided into two equal halves, light and dark. This is unlike the basic log cabin block, in which one side is always larger than the other.

Although a dark solid fabric is often chosen for the cornerstones, consider also light fabrics and prints, or even multicolored cornerstones. It is necessary only that the cornerstone fabric(s) contrast with both the light and dark halves of the log cabin block.

Unlike special logs in accent colors, which produce secondary designs, the cornerstones outline and accent the overall design of the quilt. Cornerstones are most effective in designs where they produce long unbroken lines, such as this Straight Furrows.

In the more complicated design below, cornerstones may add unnecessary fussiness.

To continue the design, the center of the log cabin block is also cut from the cornerstone fabric. Large centers, illustrated at right, make an attractive variation.

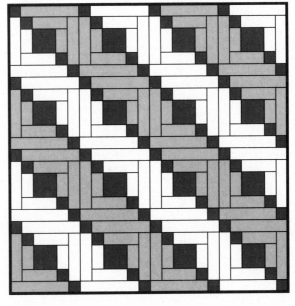

Construction techniques

The cornerstones are strip pieced onto either all the dark or all the light logs before the block is pieced. It does not matter whether the cornerstones are attached to the light or the dark logs; from the front it is impossible to tell which were used.

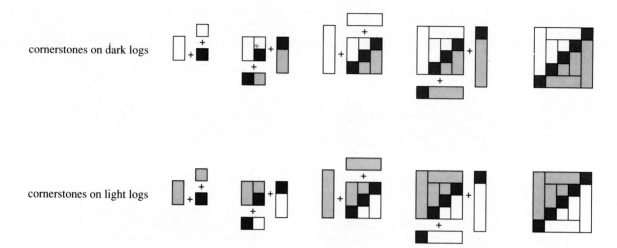

cornerstones on dark logs

cornerstones on light logs

If you plan to make only one side of the block scrappy, attach the cornerstones to the unscrappy side. It speeds things up considerably if you can speed piece the cornerstones *en masse*.

The log lengths on one side of the block must each be shortened by one finished log width, to accommodate the square cornerstones. Some sample Chimneys and Cornerstones cut measurements:

basic log cabin dark logs	Chimneys and Cornerstones dark logs	cornerstones
1 ½" x 2 ½"	1 ½" x 1 ½"	1 ½" x 1 ½"
1 ½" x 3 ½"	1 ½" x 2 ½"	1 ½" x 1 ½"
1 ½" x 4 ½"	1 ½" x 3 ½"	1 ½" x 1 ½"
1 ½" x 5 ½"	1 ½" x 4 ½"	1 ½" x 1 ½"

Logs and cornerstones are not actually cut to these measurements; you do not want to sew each cornerstone individually to each log. Instead, construct a strip unit of log fabric plus cornerstone fabric for each log position, and crosscut the logs from it.

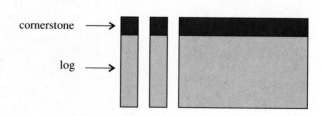

cornerstone

log

The length of the strip units depends on how many logs you need to cut from each one. There will be one log of each size in each block, so the number of logs you need to crosscut from each strip unit is equal to the number of blocks in your quilt. Using our same sample block, if you need 16 blocks you will need 16 crosscuts each 1 ¹/₂" wide, or 24" total. Add at least an inch for leeway. Cut the fabric for the first log 25" x 1 ¹/₂", the fabric for the second log 25" x 2 ¹/₂", etc. Cut the cornerstone strips 25" x 1 ¹/₂"; the cornerstone strips are always the standard cut width of the logs.

The strip units for our sample block will look like these. There is a different strip unit for each log position.

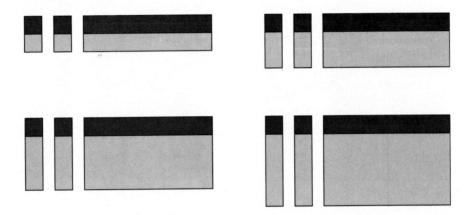

Always press the cornerstone seam allowances toward the log, away from the cornerstones. As you add each cornerstone log and match this seam to the seam in the block, the seam allowances will always be pressed in the opposite directions. This reduces bulk and allows you to carefully match the two seamlines.

Always press the corner-stone seam allowances toward the log.

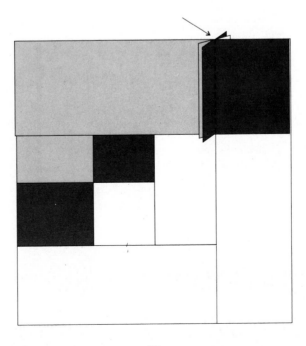

99

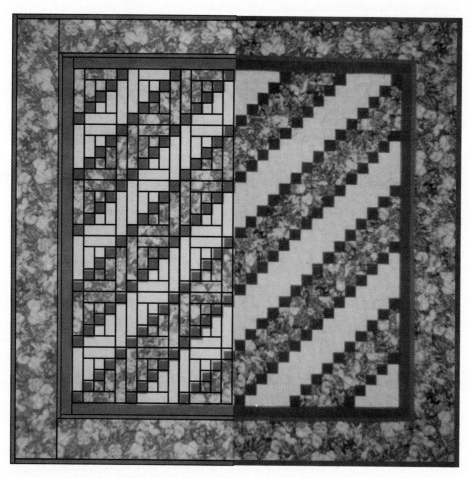

Mary's Chimneys and Cornerstones *by Mary Hales; color plate on page 78, instructions on page 101.*

Instructions: Chimneys and Cornerstones

Mary's Chimneys and Cornerstones (page 78; diagram opposite)

Mary's quilt uses the simplest version of the Chimneys and Cornerstones block: one light fabric, one dark fabric, and one cornerstone fabric. Although the cornerstones could be attached to either the dark or the light logs, follow the "cornerstones on light logs" illustration on page 98.

Quilt size	51" x 51"
Number of blocks	36
Block size	6 ¹/₄" finished
Log width	1 ¹/₄" finished
Number of rounds	2
Border	1 ¹/₄" inner border, ¹/₂" accent border, 5" outer border

Fabric required
1 yard light fabric
2 yards dark fabric (includes outer border)
1 ¹/₂ yards cornerstone fabric (includes inner border and binding)
¹/₄ yard accent fabric
2 ¹/₂ yards backing fabric
¹/₂ yard binding fabric

Cutting instructions

Centers: Strip piece the centers and the first dark logs, from 2 selvage-to-selvage cuts of cornerstone fabric and 2 similar cuts of dark fabric (see page 19). Make 36 crosscuts each 1 ³/₄" wide.

Dark logs: Cut 36 of each log from the dark fabric. (The first dark log has already been strip pieced.)
    1 ³/₄" x 3"
    1 ³/₄" x 4 ¹/₄"
    1 ³/₄" x 5 ¹/₂"

Borders:
From the cornerstone fabric, cut 2 strips
    1 ³/₄" x 38" and 2 strips 1 ³/₄" x 40 ¹/₂".
From the accent fabric, cut 2 strips 1" x
    40 ¹/₂" and 2 strips 1" x 41 ¹/₂".
From the dark fabric, cut 2 strips 5 ¹/₂" x
    41 ¹/₂", and piece 2 strips 5 ¹/₂" x 51 ¹/₂".

Cornerstone logs: Make 2 selvage-to-selvage cuts of each width listed from the light fabric. (NOTE: If your fabrics are more than 42" wide and you cut carefully, you can get enough crosscuts from 1 ¹/₂ strip units rather than the 2 in these directions.)
    1 ³/₄"
    3"
    4 ¹/₄"
    5 ¹/₂"
Make 8 selvage-to-selvage cuts of cornerstone fabric 1 ³/₄" wide. Sew a strip of cornerstone fabric to each background cut. Press seam allowances away from the cornerstones. Crosscut 36 logs from each set of strip units.

Frances's Chimneys and Cornerstones (page 78)

The cornerstones are added to the light logs; the dark logs are made from two different fabrics, one for each round. Follow the "cornerstones on light logs" illustration on page 98.

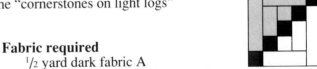

Quilt size	43" x 43"
Number of blocks	36
Block size	6 ¹/₄" finished
Log width	1 ¹/₄" finished
Number of rounds	2
Border	2 ¹/₂"

Fabric required
¹/₂ yard dark fabric A
³/₄ yard dark fabric B
1 yard light fabric
1 ¹/₄ yard cornerstone fabric (includes border)
1 ¹/₂ yards backing fabric
¹/₂ yard binding fabric

Cutting instructions

Follow instructions for Mary's Chimneys and Cornerstones, cutting the first two dark logs from fabric A and the second two from fabric B.

Border: From the cornerstones fabric, cut 2 strips 3" x 37 ¹/₂" and 2 strips 3" x 43 ¹/₂" (piece if necessary).

Yellow Chimneys and Cornerstones (page 80)

The cornerstones are added to the light logs; the dark logs are scrappy. Follow the "cornerstones on light logs" illustration on page 98.

		Fabric required
Quilt size	37" x 31"	1 yard total dark fabrics
Number of blocks	30	1 yard light fabric
Block size	6 $\frac{1}{4}$" finished	$\frac{1}{2}$ yard cornerstone fabric
Log width	1 $\frac{1}{4}$" finished	1 yard backing fabric
Number of rounds	2	$\frac{1}{2}$ yard binding fabric

Cutting instructions

Follow the directions for Mary's Chimneys and Cornerstones, cutting for 30 blocks instead of 36 and constructing 1 $\frac{1}{2}$ strip units instead of 2 strip units. Instead of speed piecing the centers, cut 36 centers from cornerstone fabric 1 $\frac{3}{4}$" x 1 $\frac{3}{4}$" and add a log the same size to the list of dark logs. Cut the dark logs from a variety of fabrics. Omit the border.

The Gerbil Quilt (page 79)

The blocks are constructed in groups of four, each group with a different dark fabric. Because there are several different darks, it is easiest to attach the cornerstones to the light fabric. Follow the "cornerstones on light logs" illustration on page 98.

		Fabric required
Quilt size	48" x 48"	$\frac{1}{4}$ yard each of 9 dark prints
Number of blocks	36	1 yard background fabric
Block size	6 $\frac{1}{4}$" finished	1 yard cornerstone fabric (includes inner
Log width	1 $\frac{1}{4}$" finished	border and corner squares)
Number of rounds	2	$\frac{3}{4}$ yard border fabric
Border	$\frac{1}{2}$" inner border,	2 yards backing fabric
	5" outer border	$\frac{1}{2}$ yard binding fabric

Cutting instructions

Follow the directions for Mary's Chimneys and Cornerstones. Cut 4 sets of dark logs from each of the 9 dark prints. Instead of speed piecing the centers, cut 36 centers from cornerstone fabric 1 $\frac{3}{4}$" x 1 $\frac{3}{4}$" and 4 dark logs the same size from each of the 9 dark prints.

Inner border: From the cornerstone fabric, cut 2 strips 1" x 38" and 2 strips 1" x 39".
Outer border: From the border fabric, cut 4 strips 5 $\frac{1}{2}$" x 39". Cut 4 squares of cornerstone fabric, 5 $\frac{1}{2}$" x 5 $\frac{1}{2}$". Sew 2 squares to each end of two of the border strips. Sew the short border strips to two sides of the quilt, then the border/corner square strips to the top and bottom.

Bigger and Better (page 82)

In this quilt the cornerstones are added to the light logs because the dark logs are scrappier. Karen actually used only one dark fabric, an unusual reversible print, and used the two sides randomly. You can substitute either one dark fabric or a scrappy collection. The cornerstone fabric is also used for two of the light logs, making an interesting secondary design. Follow the "cornerstones on light logs" illustration on page 98.

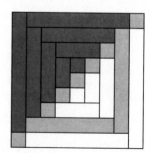

		Fabric required
Quilt size	80" x 103"	3 $\frac{3}{4}$ yards dark fabric
Number of blocks	48	5 yards light fabric (includes
Block size	11 $\frac{1}{4}$" finished	border)
Log width	1 $\frac{1}{4}$" finished	2 $\frac{1}{2}$ yards cornerstones fabric
Number of rounds	4	7 yards backing fabric
Border	6 $\frac{1}{2}$"	$\frac{3}{4}$ yard binding fabric

Cutting instructions

Centers: Strip piece the centers and the first dark logs, from 2 selvage-to-selvage cuts of cornerstone fabric and 2 similar cuts of dark fabric (see page 19). Make 48 crosscuts each 1 ³/₄" wide (see note under cornerstone logs).

Dark logs: Follow the measurements on page 21 for 1 ¹/₄" finished logs. Use the light measurements for the dark fabric, through 10 ¹/₂", omitting the first log. Cut 48 sets from the dark fabric.

Cornerstone logs: You may need only 2 strip units for each log; you need 48 crosscuts and 24 x 1 ³/₄" cuts = 42". That leaves little or nothing for cleanup cuts and miscuts. The fabric yardages allow enough fabric for 2 ¹/₂ strip units, but you will probably need to make only 2 and then maybe piece a few more logs.

To construct the strip units, make 2 selvage-to-selvage cuts of each width listed from the light fabric.
- 1 ³/₄"
- 3"
- 4 ¹/₄"
- 5 ¹/₂"
- 9 ¹/₄"
- 10 ¹/₂"

Make 12 cuts each 1 ³/₄" wide of the cornerstone fabric. Sew a strip to each cut of light fabric, and press the seam allowances away from the cornerstone strips. Make 48 crosscuts from each set of strip units.

Cut 48 sets of logs from the cornerstone fabric for the accent logs.
- 1 ³/₄" x 8"
- 1 ³/₄" x 9 ¹/₄"

Border: Piece 2 strips 7" x 90 ¹/₂" for the sides and 2 strips 7" x 81" for the top and bottom.

Cornered V's (page 80)

Cornerstones needn't be dark or solid colors; these cornerstones cut from a large-scale flower print fabric really sparkle. The cornerstones are added to the dark logs; the light logs are scrappy. Follow the "cornerstones on dark logs" illustration on page 98.

Quilt size	40" x 54"
Number of blocks	24
Block size	7" finished
Log width	1" finished
Number of rounds	3
Border	6"

Fabric required
- 1 yard dark fabric
- 1 yard total light fabrics
- 1 ¹/₂ yards cornerstone fabric (includes border)
- 1 ³/₄ yards backing fabric
- ¹/₂ yard binding fabric

Cutting instructions

Centers: Cut 24 from cornerstone fabric, 1 ¹/₂" x 1 ¹/₂".

Light logs: Using the measurements on page 21 for 1" finished logs, cut 24 sets from a variety of light fabrics, through 6 ¹/₂".

Cornerstone logs: Make a selvage-to-selvage cut in each of the widths listed.
- 1 ¹/₂"
- 2 ¹/₂"
- 3 ¹/₂"
- 4 ¹/₂"
- 5 ¹/₂"
- 6 ¹/₂"

Make 6 cuts each 1 ¹/₂" wide of cornerstone fabric. Sew a strip to each cut of dark fabric, and press the seam allowances away from the cornerstone strips. Make 24 crosscuts from each strip unit.

Border: Cut 2 strips 6 ¹/₂" x 40 ¹/₂" and 2 strips 6 ¹/₂" x 42 ¹/₂".

Rectangular Chimneys and Cornerstones (page 79)

Follow the "cornerstones on light logs" illustrations on page 98. Half of the blocks are constructed clockwise and half counterclockwise. The border is speed-pieced.

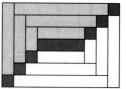

		Fabric required
Quilt size	58" x 76"	1 $\frac{1}{4}$ yards fabric A
Number of blocks	36	$\frac{3}{4}$ yard fabric B
Block size	7" x 10" finished	1 $\frac{1}{2}$ yards fabric C
Log width	1" finished	1 yard cornerstone fabric
Number of rounds	3	(includes accent border)
Border	1" accent border	4 $\frac{1}{2}$ yards background fabric
	2" background spacer	(includes border)
	2 $\frac{3}{8}$" speed-pieced border	4 $\frac{1}{2}$ yards backing fabric
	1 $\frac{1}{2}$" background spacer	$\frac{3}{4}$ yard binding fabric
	1" outer border	

Cutting instructions

Centers: Speed piece the centers and the first dark logs, from 4 selvage-to-selvage cuts of cornerstone fabric and 4 similar cuts of dark fabric A (see page 19). Make 36 crosscuts each 4 $\frac{1}{2}$" wide.

Dark logs: Cut 36 sets from the fabrics listed. The logs are listed in the order they are added to the block.

1 $\frac{1}{2}$" x 4 $\frac{1}{2}$"	fabric A
1 $\frac{1}{2}$" x 2 $\frac{1}{2}$"	fabric A
1 $\frac{1}{2}$" x 6 $\frac{1}{2}$"	fabric B
1 $\frac{1}{2}$" x 4 $\frac{1}{2}$"	fabric B
1 $\frac{1}{2}$" x 8 $\frac{1}{2}$"	fabric C
1 $\frac{1}{2}$" x 6 $\frac{1}{2}$"	fabric C

Cornerstone logs: From the background fabric, make 1 $\frac{1}{2}$ selvage-to-selvage cuts of each width listed.

4 $\frac{1}{2}$"
2 $\frac{1}{2}$"
6 $\frac{1}{2}$"
4 $\frac{1}{2}$"
8 $\frac{1}{2}$"
6 $\frac{1}{2}$"

Make 9 selvage-to-selvage cuts of the cornerstone fabric, each 1 $\frac{1}{2}$" wide. Cut 3 in half. Add a strip of cornerstone fabric to each full and half cut of background fabric. Press all seam allowances toward the log fabric, away from the cornerstones. Make 36 crosscuts 1 $\frac{1}{2}$" wide from each set of strip units.

Remember to piece half of the blocks clockwise and half counterclockwise.

BORDERS

Inner accent border: Cut 2 strips 1 $\frac{1}{2}$" x 42 $\frac{1}{2}$" and piece 2 strips 1 $\frac{1}{2}$" x 62 $\frac{1}{2}$" from the cornerstone fabric.

Inner spacer border: Piece 2 strips 2 $\frac{1}{2}$" x 44 $\frac{1}{2}$" and 2 strips 2 $\frac{1}{2}$" x 66 $\frac{1}{2}$" from the background fabric.

Outer spacer border: Piece 2 strips 2" x 53 $\frac{1}{4}$" and 2 strips 2" x 74 $\frac{1}{4}$" from the background fabric.

Outer dark border: Piece 2 strips 1 $\frac{1}{2}$" x 56 $\frac{1}{4}$" and 2 strips 1 $\frac{1}{2}$" x 76 $\frac{1}{4}$" from fabric A. (You could omit this border and substitute a wide dark binding.)

For the speed-pieced border, make 1 $\frac{1}{2}$"-wide selvage-to-selvage cuts, 9 of fabric A and 8 of fabric C. Make 34 cuts of background fabric 1 $\frac{3}{4}$" wide. Make 17 strip units as shown, 9 with fabric A and 8 with fabric C. Press seam allowances *toward* fabric A and *away from* fabric C.

press seam allowances toward fabric A

press seam allowances away from fabric C

Make 120 crosscuts from fabric A strip units and 116 from fabric C strip units, all 1 $\frac{1}{2}$" wide. *Make all cuts at a 45° angle.* Half of the crosscuts of each type should angle to the right, and half to the left. You can accomplish this easily by matching the strip units in pairs, *wrong sides together*, and making the crosscuts two at a time.

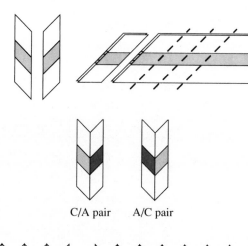

Seam A and C crosscuts together into 112 pairs, 56 in C/A pairs as shown on the left and 56 in A/C pairs as shown on the right.

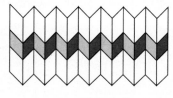

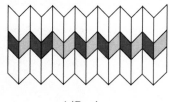

C/A pair   A/C pair

For each of the two short-side pieced borders, seam together 12 C/A pairs and 12 A/C pairs (= 48 diamonds). Join them together. In the center there will be two adjoining A diamonds, and each border will begin and end with a C diamond.

For the two long-side pieced borders, seam together 16 C/A pairs, and 16 A/C pairs (= 64 diamonds). Piece two C/C pairs and place one in the center of each border (= 66 diamonds). Each border will begin and end with a C diamond.

C/A pairs   A/C pairs

Press all seam allowances in one direction. Press carefully so you don't distort the bias edges.

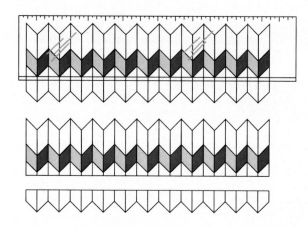

To trim the borders, lay your 24" acrylic rotary ruler along one long edge of the border, with the $\frac{1}{4}$" line along the points of the A and C diamonds. Trim away the excess background fabric, leaving a $\frac{1}{4}$" seam allowance. Repeat on the other long edge. Handle each border carefully; the long edges are all bias and will easily stretch out of shape.

Rip the seam and remove the background fabric from one edge of the remaining 8 A crosscuts. Cut 4 squares from background fabric, 1 $\frac{7}{8}$" x 1 $\frac{7}{8}$". Piece and trim 4 corner blocks as shown below.

Sew the corner blocks to the ends of the longer border strips.

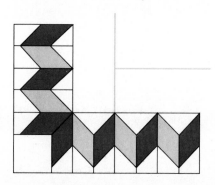

Add all border strips to the short sides first, then the long sides of the quilt. Add the borders to the quilt in this order (finished measurements): 1" cornerstone fabric, 2" background fabric, pieced border, 1 $\frac{1}{2}$" background fabric, 1" dark fabric (or dark binding).

This quilt is a considerably more complicated version of Deep Purple Dreams (page 29). The central part of the quilt, however, is remarkably simple; the interwoven design is composed of only two different Chimneys and Cornerstones blocks, shown at right. Bringing in a third color, as I did, increases the number of different blocks only to four. For a diagram of the design without cornerstones, see page 31.

The difficulty with this piece is in the outer round of blocks. There are seven more kinds of log cabin blocks in the outer round, and some of them are pretty odd.

If you wish to keep the outer round but still simplify the quilt, you could use one background fabric instead of a scrappy variety; this greatly speeds up the cutting. The subtle scrappy effect in the ribbons is lovely but time-consuming, particularly with a Chimneys and Cornerstones quilt. Eliminating the cornerstones and using basic log cabin blocks instead, as in Deep Purple Dreams and its variations, also saves much time.

I quilted in white down the center of each white log, and in black down the centers of the ribbons, each in a different continuous design.

Quilt size	60" x 76"
Number of blocks	72
Block size	7" finished
Log width	1" finished
Number of rounds	3
Border	2" inner border (top and bottom only), 2" outer border

Fabric required
- 1 ½ yards total green fabrics
- ⅔ yard green cornerstone fabric
- 1 ¼ yards total teal fabrics
- ½ yard teal cornerstone fabric
- 1 ¼ yards total fuchsia fabrics
- ½ yard fuchsia cornerstone fabric
- 2 ½ yards total white-on-white fabrics (includes inner border)
- ¾ yard outer border fabric
- 4 yards backing fabric
- ¾ yard binding fabric

Cutting instructions

NOTE: The directions for the cornerstone logs are written as if you are working with only one fabric in each log position. If you are working with a scrappy variety of fabrics, cut shorter lengths and make three or four shorter strip units for each cornerstone log.

Centers: Cut 1 ½" x 1 ½" center squares from the fabrics listed.

32	green cornerstone fabric
12	teal cornerstone fabric
12	fuchsia cornerstone fabric
16	white fabrics

White logs
1. Make a selvage-to-selvage cut in each width listed.
    - 1 ½"
    - 3 ½"
    - 5 ½"

    Make 3 selvage-to-selvage cuts 1 ½" wide from green cornerstone fabric. Sew one to each cut of white to make strip units. Make 24 crosscuts from each strip unit for cornerstone logs.

2. Cut the number of each log indicated. You may cut some of the smaller logs from the left-over pieces of the cornerstone-log strip units.

48	1 ½" x 1 ½"
42	1 ½" x 2 ½"
64	1 ½" x 3 ½"
42	1 ½" x 4 ½"
64	1 ½" x 5 ½"
42	1 ½" x 6 ½"
16	1 ½" x 7 ½"

Green logs

1. Make a selvage-to-selvage cut in each width listed.

    1 ½"
    2 ½"
    3 ½"
    4 ½"
    5 ½"
    6 ½"

    Make 6 selvage-to-selvage cuts 1 ½" wide from green cornerstone fabric. Sew one to each cut of green to make strip units. Make 24 crosscuts from the first, third, and fifth strip units for cornerstone logs. Make 32 crosscuts from the second, fourth, and sixth strip units. (You will not be able to make all 32 from one strip unit. Piece the last few from individual logs and cornerstone squares.)

2. Cut 24 logs of each size listed.

    1 ½" x 1 ½"
    1 ½" x 3 ½"
    1 ½" x 5 ½"

Teal logs

Use the cornerstone log measurements from the green logs, above. Make a selvage-to-selvage cut in each of the first, third, and fifth widths. Make ½ a selvage-to-selvage cut in each of the second, fourth, and sixth widths (that is, construct strip units that are 20" long instead of 40").

Make 3 selvage-to-selvage cuts and 3 cuts 20" long of teal cornerstone fabric, 1 ½" wide. Sew to the teal pieces to make strip units. Make 28 crosscuts from the long strip units and 12 crosscuts from the short strip units.

Fuchsia logs

Follow the directions for the teal logs. Make 26 crosscuts from the long strip units and 12 crosscuts from the short strip units.

Piecing instructions

Piece blocks A-H in the quantities and colors listed below. In the illustrations of the blocks (next page), the darkest shades are always green. The medium shades are either teal or fuchsia.

Each block is drawn in the same position: the first log added is drawn above the center, the next to the left, the next below the center, and so on, around the block counterclockwise. The two sides of the block are here referred to as "upper" and "lower".

upper

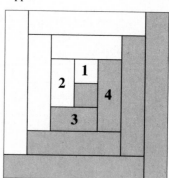

lower

quantity		upper	lower
10	A	white + teal cornerstone	green cornerstone
10	A	white + fuchsia cornerstone	green cornerstone
12	B	green + white cornerstone	teal cornerstone
12	B	green + white cornerstone	fuchsia cornerstone
2	C	white	green cornerstone
6	D	white (no cornerstones)	white (no cornerstones)
2	E	white + teal cornerstone	white + green cornerstone
8	F	white	white + green cornerstone
2	G	white + green cornerstone	white
4	H	white + teal cornerstone	white
4	H	white + fuchsia cornerstone	white

72 blocks

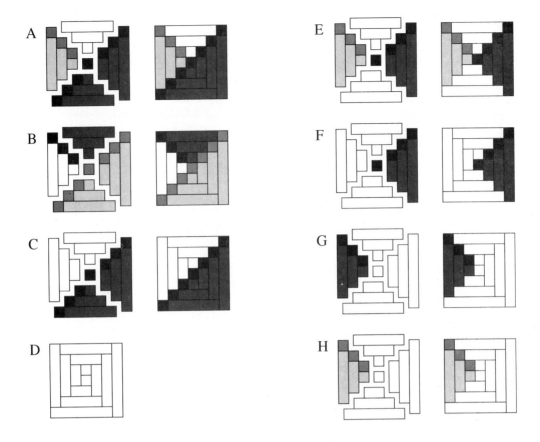

Follow the diagram and the color photograph of the quilt for placement of the blocks. The circled blocks have fuchsia in place of teal.

Inner border: Piece 4 white strips 1 ½" x 56 ½". Add 2 strips to the top of the quilt, and 2 to the bottom. (If you are using one white fabric, piece 2 strips 2 ½" x 56 ½" and add one to the top and one to the bottom.) There are no inner border strips on the sides.

Outer border: Piece 2 strips 2 ½" x 56 ½" and 2 strips 2 ½" x 76 ½".

D	Ⓗ	Ⓑ	E	A	F	G	D
Ⓗ	Ⓐ	B	Ⓐ	A	A	C	D
F	Ⓐ	Ⓑ	Ⓐ	Ⓐ	A	B	F
H	B	Ⓑ	Ⓑ	Ⓐ	Ⓑ	B	H
F	B	B	Ⓑ	Ⓐ	Ⓑ	Ⓑ	F
H	A	B	A	Ⓐ	Ⓐ	Ⓑ	Ⓗ
F	A	B	A	A	Ⓐ	Ⓑ	F
D	C	B	B	A	B	Ⓑ	Ⓗ
D	G	F	B	E	B	H	D

109

Three Hearts by Marilyn Bacon; color plate on page 85, instructions on page 119.

Thick-and-Thin

The traditional log cabin block is constructed of logs of equal width. If all of the logs on one side of the block are thinner than the logs on the other side of the block, the two sides of the block are divided by a curved line.

The relationship between the widths of the two types of logs determines the deepness of the curve.

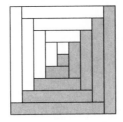 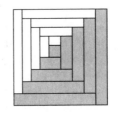 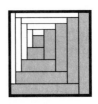

thick to thin: 1 : 1 1 : $^3/_4$ 1 : $^1/_2$ 1 : $^1/_4$

When the thin logs are half the width of the thick logs, a gentle curve results. All of the thick and thin projects in this book use this proportion.

To emphasize the curved line, you may want to de-emphasize the stairstep effect all log cabin blocks have. The stairstep effect can be reduced in the curved line by increasing the number of rounds or decreasing the width of the logs, although anything narrower than 1" thick and $^1/_2$" thin is difficult to sew. The stairstep effect is most pronounced when solid, high-contrast fabrics are used for the light and dark halves of the block; it is reduced when prints are used for both sides of the block. See page 11.

To maintain the curve, the center square is generally not emphasized; it should be treated as just another dark or light log.

The curved lines, of course, do interesting things to the traditional log cabin designs.

As it happens, the curve of 1 : $^1/_2$ Thick-and-Thin blocks is very similar to the curve of Joyce Schlotzhauer's curved two-patch designs.* Her books are good sources of design ideas for Thick-and-Thin quilts.

*The Curved Two-Patch System, Curves Unlimited, and Cutting Up with Curves by Joyce Schlotzhauer, EPM Publications. These books may be out of print and difficult to find.

Construction techniques

Thick-and-Thin log cabin blocks are constructed in the same manner as regular log cabin blocks. The block is easiest to start if the center is a thick square. If you work in full rounds and start with a pair of thin logs, the final pair of logs will be thick. If you start with a pair of thick logs, the final pair of logs will be thin.

thick outer logs

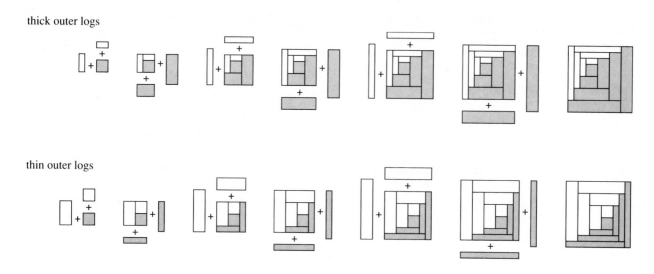

thin outer logs

The final pair of logs, thick or thin, will extend to the edges of the block and, in many designs, touch the same outer logs in adjoining blocks. This may be an important consideration as you design a Thick-and-Thin quilt.

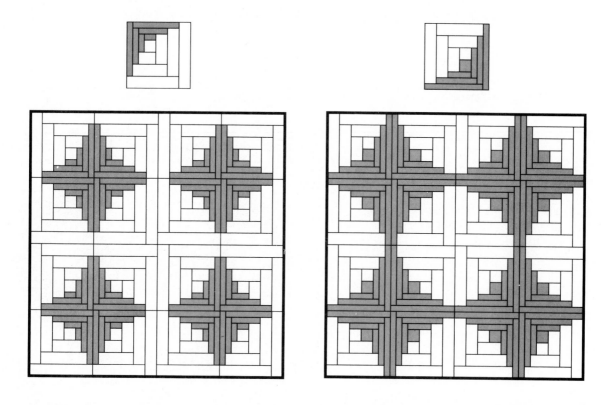

Instructions: Thick-and-Thin

Four Suns (page 84)

Purchase a series of hand-dyed fabrics for this wall hanging, or select a shaded series of fabrics. Machine-quilted circles echo the curved lines of the log cabin blocks. Follow the "thin outer logs" illustration on page 112.

		Fabric required
Quilt size	38" x 38"	
Number of blocks	16	2 sets of fat $1/8$ yards of 8 shades,
Block size	7" finished	or $1/4$ yard each of 8 shades
Log width	1", $1/2$" finished	$3/4$ yard border fabric
Number of rounds	4	1 $1/4$ yards backing fabric
Border	5"	$1/2$ yard binding fabric

Cutting instructions

Line up the eight fabrics and letter them, from darkest A to lightest H. Each fabric is used for a pair of thick (light) or thin (dark) logs. Fabric D is used for a pair of thin logs and for the centers. Cut and stack the logs in the order listed.

Centers: Cut 16 squares 1 $1/2$" x 1 $1/2$" from fabric D.

Thick logs: Cut 16 sets from the fabric listed.   *Thin logs:* Cut 16 sets from the fabric listed.

E	1 $1/2$" x 1 $1/2$"	G	1 $1/2$" x 4 $1/2$"	D	1" x 2 $1/2$"	B	1" x 5 $1/2$"
E	1 $1/2$" x 2 $1/2$"	G	1 $1/2$" x 5 $1/2$"	D	1" x 3"	B	1" x 6"
F	1 $1/2$" x 3"	H	1 $1/2$" x 6"	C	1" x 4"	A	1" x 7"
F	1 $1/2$" x 4"	H	1 $1/2$" x 7"	C	1" x 4 $1/2$"	A	1" x 7 $1/2$"

Border: Cut 2 strips 5 $1/2$" x 28 $1/2$" and 2 strips 5 $1/2$" x 38 $1/2$".

Christmas Wreath (page 84)

The red centers of the green and white blocks look like holly berries on the wreath design. Follow the "thick outer logs" illustration on page 112.

		Fabric required
Quilt size	42" x 42"	$1/2$ yard total green prints
Number of blocks	16	$1/2$ yard total light prints
Block size	7" finished	$1/4$ yard total red prints
Log width	1", $1/2$" finished	$1/3$ yard inner border
Number of rounds	4	$3/4$ yard outer border
Border	2" inner border,	1 $1/2$ yards backing fabric
	5" outer border	$1/2$ yard binding fabric

Cutting instructions

Thick logs: Cut 12 sets from a variety of green fabrics and 4 sets from a variety of red fabrics. Cut green centers for the red blocks, and red centers for the green blocks.

1 $1/2$" x 1 $1/2$" (center)	
1 $1/2$" x 2"	1 $1/2$" x 5"
1 $1/2$" x 3"	1 $1/2$" x 6"
1 $1/2$" x 3 $1/2$"	1 $1/2$" x 6 $1/2$"
1 $1/2$" x 4 $1/2$"	1 $1/2$" x 7 $1/2$"

Thin logs: Cut 16 sets from a variety of light fabrics.

1" x 1 $1/2$"	1" x 4 $1/2$"
1" x 2"	1" x 5"
1" x 3"	1" x 6"
1" x 3 $1/2$"	1" x 6 $1/2$"

Inner border: Cut 2 strips 2 $1/2$" x 28 $1/2$" and 2 strips 2 $1/2$" x 32 $1/2$".

Outer border: Cut 2 strips 5 $1/2$" x 32 $1/2$" and 2 strips 5 $1/2$" x 42 $1/2$".

Scarlet Ribbons (page 85)

The secret to this quilt is careful fabric selection; the reds are so close that there is little difference between most of the side-by-side pairs. Lines of hand quilting accent the curves. Follow the "thick outer logs" illustration on page 112.

Quilt size   28" x 28"
Number of blocks   25
Block size   5 ¹/₂" finished
Log width   1", ¹/₂" finished
Number of rounds   3

Fabric required
10 fabrics A-J, with A the lightest and
    J the darkest
¹/₈ yard each A, B, H, I, and J
¹/₄ yard each C, D, E, F, and G
1 yard backing fabric
¹/₂ yard binding fabric

Cutting instructions
Follow the log measurements for Christmas Wreath, omitting the last two thick logs and the last two thin logs.
Cut sets of logs from each fabric as listed.

fabric	thick sets	thin sets
A	1	0
B	1	2
C	3	2
D	3	4
E	5	4
F	4	5
G	4	3
H	2	3
I	2	1
J	0	1

Following the diagrams, piece 25 blocks. There are so many different combinations that you will probably want to piece most of the blocks one by one. Set up a table right next to you with your iron and a folded terrycloth towel, so you can press each seam after you sew it without having to jump up and go to your ironing board.

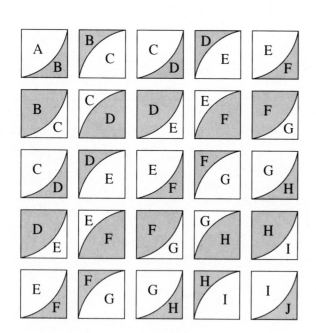

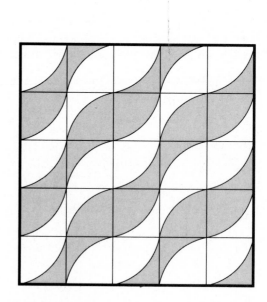

114

Log Cabin Variation (page 83)

Follow the "thick outer logs" illustration on page 112 but add only 3 ¹/₂ rounds to the center, ending with thin outer logs instead of thick.

Quilt size	43" x 43"
Number of blocks	36
Block size	6"
Log width	1", ¹/₂"
Number of rounds	3 ¹/₂
Border	1 ¹/₄" inner border, ¹/₄" accent border, 2" outer border

Fabric required
³/₄ yard total dark fabrics
1 ¹/₄ yards total light fabrics
¹/₈ yard red fabric
¹/₃ yard inner border fabric
¹/₈ yard accent border fabric
¹/₂ yard outer border fabric
1 ¹/₂ yards backing fabric
¹/₂ yard binding fabric

Cutting instructions
Follow the log measurements for Christmas Wreath, omitting the last two thick logs.
Cut 36 sets of logs. Cut the thick logs from light fabrics and the thin logs from dark fabrics. Cut the centers from red fabric.

Inner border: Cut 2 strips 1 ³/₄" x 36 ¹/₂" and 2 strips 1 ³/₄" x 39".
Accent border: Cut 2 strips ¹/₂" x 39" and 2 strips ¹/₂" x 39 ¹/₂".
Outer border: Cut 2 strips 2 ¹/₂" x 39 ¹/₂" and 2 strips 2 ¹/₂" x 43 ¹/₂".

Pinks and Purples (page 82)

To achieve the undulating lines of this design, some blocks use dark fabrics for the thick logs, and some use dark fabrics for the thin logs. Follow the "thin outer logs" illustration on page 112.

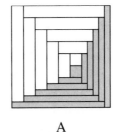   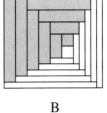

A   B

Quilt size	51" x 59"
Number of blocks	42
Block size	8 ¹/₂" finished
Log width	1", ¹/₂" finished
Number of rounds	5

Fabric required
2 ¹/₂ yards total dark fabrics
2 ¹/₄ yards light fabric
3 yards backing fabric
¹/₂ yard binding fabric

Cutting instructions
Follow the measurements for Four Suns, adding two more thick logs (1 ¹/₂" x 7 ¹/₂", 1 ¹/₂" x 8 ¹/₂") and two more thin logs (1" x 8 ¹/₂", 1" x 9").

From the light fabric, cut 28 sets of thick logs and 14 sets of thin logs. From a variety of dark fabrics, cut 14 sets of thick logs and 28 sets of thin logs. Piece 28 A blocks and 14 B blocks. Follow the diagram for placement of the A and B blocks.

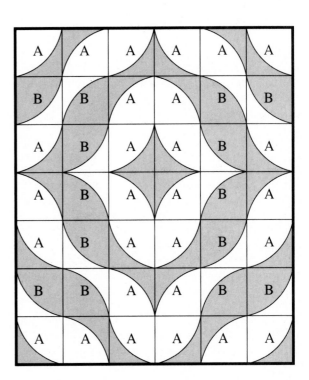

The lovely braid border is easily speed-pieced; the hard part of a braid border is figuring out the measurements, and I have already done that for you. To piece the blocks, follow the "thin outer logs" illustration on page 112.

		Fabric required
Quilt size	42" x 42"	1 ³/₄ yards total purple fabrics
Number of blocks	16	(includes pieced border)
Block size	7" finished	1 yard background fabric (includes
Log width	1", ¹/₂" finished	inner border)
Number of rounds	4	¹/₂ yard total green fabrics
Border	2" inner border,	1 yard accent border fabric (includes
	1" accent border,	1" binding)
	3 ¹/₂" pieced border	1 ¹/₃ yards backing fabric

Cutting instructions

Follow the measurements for Four Suns. From a variety of purple fabrics, cut 8 sets of thick logs and 4 sets of thin logs. From a variety of green fabrics, cut 4 sets of thick logs and 2 sets of thin logs. From the background fabric, cut 4 sets of thick logs and 10 sets of thin logs.

Piece the quantity of each block listed and follow the diagram for placement of the blocks.

6 A
2 B
2 C
2 D
4 E

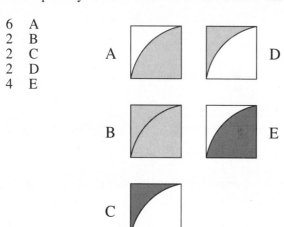

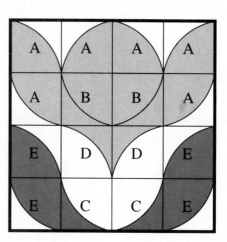

Inner border: Cut 2 strips 2 ¹/₂" x 28 ¹/₂" and 2 strips 2 ¹/₂" x 32 ¹/₂". NOTE: Prepare the braid border before you cut the inner and accent borders. You may need to modify the width of the inner border so that *your* braid will fit.

Accent border: Cut 2 strips 1 ¹/₂" x 32 ¹/₂" and 2 strips 1 ¹/₂" x 34 ¹/₂". See note for inner border.

Braid border

Make 35 selvage-to-selvage cuts of a variety of fabrics, each 1 ¹/₄" wide. Sew the strips together in different combinations into 5 strip units, each 7 strips wide. Your strip unit should be 5 ³/₄" wide, including seam allowances. Crosscut your strip units into 5 ³/₄" squares. Cut each square diagonally into two triangles, reversing the direction of the diagonal with each cut. Make 10 pairs of diagonal cuts in this manner, then make 2 additional diagonal cuts like the first one on the left. This makes 32 squares and 64 triangles.

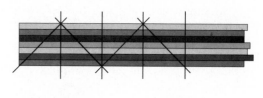

Make two stacks of triangles. The ones on the left are the mirror image of the ones on the right. The stack on the left should have 20 triangles, and the stack on the right 24 triangles.

Piece together nine triangles into a border strip, as shown. Repeat for the other three borders. Pull the first triangle from the left pile, the next from the right pile, then back to the left pile, and so on. Mix up the triangles from different strip units so your border looks scrappy. The diagonal seam is a little tricky; see page 126 for some hints.

Piece two of the remaining triangles for each of the four corners.

Measure your border strips along the longest edge, from tip to tip. If they are 35 $^1/_4$" long, you are right on the button. If they are $^1/_2$" or so too big or too small, you are probably still okay because this border is all bias edges and can be stretched or eased quite a bit. If you are off by more, modify your inner and accent borders accordingly: increase or decrease the *width* of each border strip by *half* the amount you are off.

Binding: Make 5 selvage-to-selvage cuts each 2 $^3/_4$" wide for 1" finished binding (see page 153).

Three Hearts (page 85)

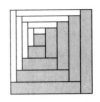

I admit I was rather stunned when Marilyn pieced 26 Thick-and-Thin blocks entirely from background fabric to make a border for the 28-block center, but she wanted to float the hearts on the same flurried background throughout the quilt, and the result is certainly handsome. Follow the "thick outer logs" illustration on page 112.

Quilt size	42" x 63"	
Number of blocks	54 (28 with plain borders)	
Block size	7" finished	
Log width	1", $^1/_2$" finished	
Number of rounds	4	
Border	7" pieced or plain	

Fabric required
$^2/_3$ yard each of three fabrics
2 $^3/_4$ yards background fabric (1 $^3/_4$ yards if you omit the pieced border)
1 $^3/_4$ yards backing fabric
$^1/_2$ yard binding fabric

Cutting instructions
Follow the measurements for Christmas Wreath. From each fabric, cut 8 sets of thick logs and 4 sets of thin logs. From the background fabric, cut 30 sets of thick logs and 42 sets of thin logs. (If you are not piecing the border, from the background fabric cut only 4 sets of thick logs and 16 sets of thin logs, and piece only 2 blocks entirely from background fabric, instead of 28.)

Piece the quantity of each block listed, and follow the diagram for placement of the blocks.

quantity	thick	thin
6	A	background
2	A	A
4	B	background
2	B	A
2	B	B
4	C	background
2	C	B
2	C	C
2	background	C
28	background	background

Red Hot Stars; *color plate on back cover, instructions on page 132.*

Cabin Stars

Cabin Stars is one of the loveliest of the log cabin variations, inspired by a quilt by Judy Martin. To make the stars, a mitered border is added to each log cabin block. Diamonds on the ends of each border piece make eight-pointed stars when the blocks are set together.

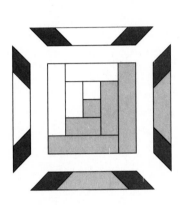

The number of rounds in the inner log cabin block determines how far apart the stars are spaced. When the stars are close together, the overall log cabin design is lost. Although the quilt on the left below is a Barn Raising and the one on the right is a Straight Furrows, they appear to be identical.

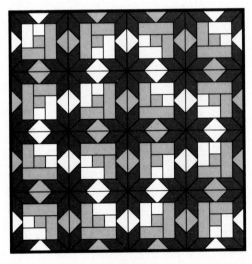

Barn Raising

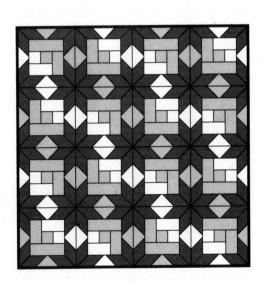

Straight Furrows

When the stars are farther
apart, they appear smaller
in proportion to the overall
design, and the quilt is
more clearly a log cabin
quilt.

The partial stars around
the edges of the quilt
design can be omitted.
This saves time when the
quilt is being pieced, but
makes the quilt more
difficult to plan because
the blocks are no longer
identical. Some blocks
have diamonds in all four
corners, some in two
corners, and some in only
one corner.

122

If you add diamonds only to opposite corners of the blocks, the stars will be staggered.

The inner log cabin block can be rectangular, as in the Christmas tree quilts on page 86. You can even do a Chimneys and Cornerstones version. Any traditional design can be made with stars between the blocks. The designs with simple lines, such as Barn Raising, Straight Furrows, and Light and Dark are most effective.

The stars create the illusion that the lines of the designs are not straight, but bumpy. In some designs the effect is quite pronounced. In the Straight-Furrows version Old Glory (page 87), the quilt has the appearance of a flag rippling in the wind.

The stars can be all from one fabric, as in Old Glory, or scrappy, as in Red Hot Stars (back cover) and Dark Stars (page 89). If you plan ahead and have your wits about you as you assemble the blocks, you can make each star from a different fabric (as in Christmas Tree #2 on page 86), or you can make each star come together in a particular design.

Construction techniques

There is no way around it: this one is difficult. I have taught this log cabin variation in many classes, however, and even beginning students have made lovely quilts. It just requires careful piecing and patience. Several tricks in this chapter will also be very helpful.

Begin by piecing all the inner log cabin blocks. These are just like any other log cabin and go together quickly.

Outer round trapezoids Once you have the inner blocks, you will prepare the logs and diamonds for the last round. If you are making all of the blocks identical, so that there are partial stars around the edges of the quilt, each block will require four outer strips: two dark, with a diamond on each end; and two light, with a diamond on each end.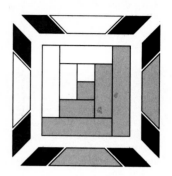

Notice that the four pieces to which the diamonds are added are all cut the same size; the only difference is that two are light and two are dark. This shape is called a trapezoid.

The angle at each end of the trapezoid is 45°. Your rotary ruler should have this angle marked on it. It is even easier to use one of the 6" square rulers marked with a diagonal; this also is a 45° angle, and the smaller ruler is less awkward.

To make each trapezoid:

1. Cut a log the same width as the others in your quilt and the length given in the instructions. The length provided is always the *cut* length of the longest edge of the trapezoid.

2. Line up the center diagonal line of your 6" square ruler on the long edge of the log, and trim each end at a 45° angle.

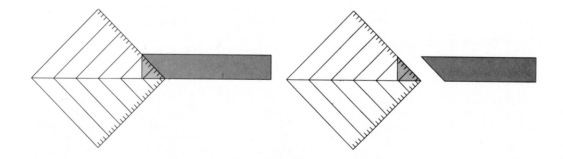

If it bothers you to waste those little triangles of fabric you trim off each end of the trapezoids, use your first trapezoid as a template (it is less slippery than a paper template; just be careful not to stretch it out of shape) and cut your trapezoids end to end. Or, measure the length with your ruler, make a tick mark, and cut at a 45° angle, reversing the direction of the cut each time to look like the illustration below.

The trapezoid measurements are correct if your inner log cabin block is exactly the right size. Since we are not machines, however, there may be slight differences, and you may need to modify the size of the trapezoid for your quilt. Sew a test block before you cut all of your trapezoids. You probably won't need to sew a whole block, as all four sides are the same; if one trapezoid unit fits, the others should fit too.

Diamonds The diamonds are very simple to cut with the 6" square ruler. On the square ruler, find the measurement on two adjoining sides that is the same as the *cut* width of the logs. Follow those two measurements to the center of the ruler, and find the point where they meet on the diagonal line. If the cut width of your logs is 1 $\frac{1}{2}$", for example, find the point on the diagonal at which the 1 $\frac{1}{2}$" lines meet. You might want to mark the point with a small piece of masking tape.

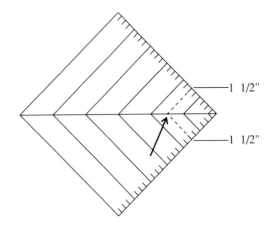

Start with a strip the cut width of the logs. Trim off one end at a 45° angle. Lay the square ruler over the end of the strip of fabric as shown, with the intersection point you just found at the inner corner of the 45° cut. Rotary cut along the edge of the ruler to make the diamond. Repeat to cut all the diamonds. You will need eight diamonds for each block in your quilt.

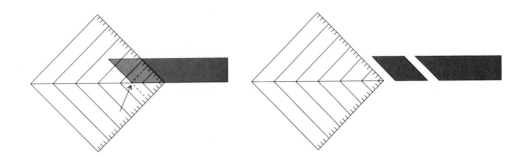

125

Attaching the diamonds   Accurately sewing the diamonds to each end of the trapezoid log is probably the trickiest step in the whole block.

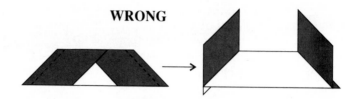

Alas, you cannot simply match points and sew. If you do, the diamonds will not lie in a straight line with the log; they will lie at a 90° angle.

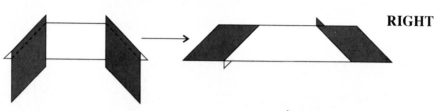

The diamonds must be attached at a 90° angle, so that when the seams are pressed the diamonds lie in a straight line with the log.

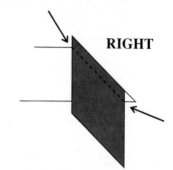

Even with the diamonds at a 90° angle, you cannot match points. The diamonds must be offset so that the ¼" seamline lies right at the point of the notch, as shown. As you begin to stitch, use the ¼" seam guide on your sewing machine. Your stitching should begin and end right at the notches.

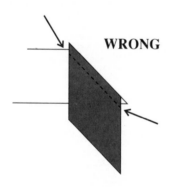

The tendency seems to be to place the diamond too low, so the little pointy piece of log peeking out at the end of the seam is too small. The correct position is tricky to get the hang of. I promise you, by the time you finish a Cabin Stars quilt you will be able to eyeball the position accurately. In the beginning, however, you may need to draw the ¼" seamline on some diamonds and pin the seam.

Once you have the diamonds attached, the seam allowances must be pressed before you attach the diamond log to the block. *Press all the diamond/trapezoid seam allowances in the same direction.*

To do this, establish a routine and follow it with each log.

1. Place the diamond log on the ironing board, wrong side up, long edge toward you.

2. Press both sets of seam allowances in the same direction.

3. Turn the log over and press again from the right side, flattening out any ridges along the seams. Be careful, however, not to stretch any bias edges out of shape.

> **Press all the diamond/trapezoid seam allowances in the same direction.**

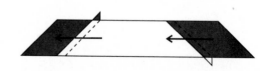

If you are left-handed, press from left to right. If you can do a good job pressing just from the front, that's fine. It doesn't matter whether you press with the long edge of the log toward you or away from you, as long as you are consistent. If you press each diamond log the same way, when you sew the blocks to each other and form the stars, each pair of diamond seam allowances will be pressed in opposite directions. This helps you line up the two seamlines accurately and reduces bulk.

Attaching the diamond logs   The next step is to attach the four diamond logs to the four sides of the inner log cabin block.

These four seams will not be sewn edge to edge; each seam will start and stop ¹/₄" from the edges. Pin the first diamond log to the log cabin block, pinning through the intersection of the seam allowance lines at each end of the seam. Be sure you sew light logs to the light sides of the block and dark logs to the dark sides.

Pin the seam once or twice in the center to keep the edges matched as you sew.

Don't match the inner corner of the diamond with the corner of the log cabin block; the corner of the diamond should lie about ¹/₈" to the inside.

Pin the first diamond log to the block, pinning through the intersection of the seam allowances at each end of the seam.

Once the ends have been pinned, if the diamond log is the proper length it should lie smoothly on the block. If it doesn't, check it on the other sides of the same block and on some other blocks. If it is consistently too long, you need to cut your trapezoid logs slightly shorter. If it is consistently too short, you need to cut your trapezoid logs slightly longer. This is why you must piece a sample block!

Attach diamond logs to two opposite sides of the block first; they are the easiest ones to do, because there is no adjacent diamond log to get in your way as you pin the corners.

Sew the seam from pin to pin, backstitching at each end for strength.

Sew a ¹/₄" seam between the end pins; do not sew over the pins. Backstitch at each end for strength. Do not press the seam allowances. The next time you will press the block will be when the mitering is all done.

The pins for the second pair of logs should go in very near the end of the seams for the first two logs. As you attach the second two diamond logs, push the diamond logs already attached out of the way, and be careful not to catch them in the seams. It is better to leave a little gap than to sew so close that you catch the adjacent diamond log.

Mitering the corners The final step in the block construction is to miter the corners. Grasp the block as shown, with the block in your left hand and the two diamonds to be mitered in your right. Pull the seam allowances at the inner corner of the diamonds out of the way, to the left.

Match the edges and outer points of the two diamonds, and pin them together near the points to keep them from slipping as you sew.

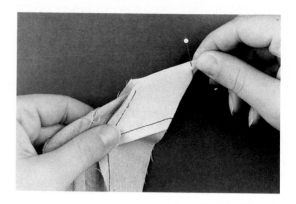

As you prepare to sew the miter seam, pull the seam allowances at the inner corner of the diamonds out of the way.

Start sewing the miter seam at the inner corner, ¹/₄" in from all the edges. Backstitch at the beginning of the seam, and make several stitches in thin air at the end of the seam to fasten it off.

Start sewing the seam at the inner corner, ¹/₄" in from all the edges. Again, it is better to leave a little gap than catch anything extraneous in the seam. Backstitch for strength at the beginning of the seam. Sew to the outer points of the diamonds, being careful not to stretch the bias edges.

It is difficult to backstitch at the outer points, on the bare edge of nothing, so instead keep sewing past the points for several machine stitches. The interlocked threads will help prevent the end of the seam from pulling open as the block is handled. Repeat the miter at the other three corners.

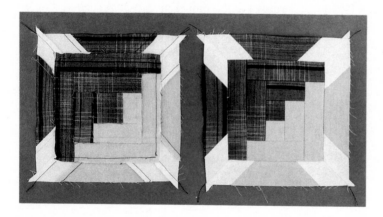

Press the mitered seams all in the same direction, clockwise or counterclockwise. Press the seams that join the final round of logs toward the logs just added, as usual.

Final pressing After all four miters are sewn, lay the block on the ironing board wrong-side up. Press the seam allowances for the outer diamond log round all toward the outer edge of the block. At each corner, press the mitered diamond seams all in the same direction. That is to say, press all the seam allowances clockwise or all counterclockwise, whichever seems a more natural movement to you.

Flip the block over from the right to wrong side and back again, and correct any seam allowances that have been scrunched or pressed in the wrong direction. See what you can do to improve the outer corners of the inner block, where the inside angles of the stars will be. There is a lot of bulk there. Pressing some of the seam allowances back toward the center of the block might help.

Corrections   Examine your completed sample block. If there are puckers at the outside corners of the inner log cabin block, where the diamonds join, you probably caught a diamond log in the seam of the adjacent log. You might want to rip out a few stitches and resew the corner.

If the outside edges of the block are rounded so the block looks slightly circular, it is probably because your seam allowance out at the points of the miters was a little too wide. In the next block, narrow the seam allowance slightly as you approach the outside point of the miter, and you should see an improvement.

If there is too much fabric along the outer edge of the block, so that the edges ripple, you need to take a slightly larger seam allowance out at the points of the miters. Try it on your next block.

Irregular outer rounds   If you construct all of your blocks with diamonds in all four corners, your quilt will have partial stars around the edges. If you want to eliminate the partial stars the outer blocks will go together more quickly, but you will spend more time planning your quilt and cutting the logs for the outer round. The length of each log in each type of outer round is given in the instructions for the quilts in this book; again, the measurement is always of the longest cut edge of the log.

Be careful when you cut the logs that have a diamond at only one end; the two examples shown here are mirror images of one another.

Straight Furrows *by Margaret Brevig; color plate on page 89, instructions on page 131.*

Instructions: Cabin Stars

Straight Furrows (page 89; diagram opposite))

Quilt size   66" x 55"
Number of blocks   20
Block size   11 $^1/_4$" finished
Log width   1 $^1/_4$" finished
Number of rounds   3 + diamond round
Border $^1/_2$" inner border,
          $^1/_2$" accent border,
          4" outer border

Fabric required
3 $^1/_4$ yards dark fabric (includes outer border
    and binding)
1 $^3/_4$ yards light fabric (incudes inner border)
1 yard star fabric (includes accent border)
3 $^1/_2$ yards backing fabric
$^1/_2$ yard binding fabric

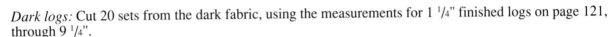

Cutting instructions

Centers: Speed piece the centers and the first light log. Make one selvage-to-selvage cut of dark fabric and one of light fabric. Sew together to make a strip unit, press the seam allowances toward the light fabric, and make 20 crosscuts each 1 $^3/_4$" wide (see page 19).

Light logs: Cut 20 sets from the light fabric, using the measurements on page 21 for 1 $^1/_4$" finished logs, starting with the 3" log and ending with the 8" log. (The first light log has already been speed-pieced.)

Dark logs: Cut 20 sets from the dark fabric, using the measurements for 1 $^1/_4$" finished logs on page 121, through 9 $^1/_4$".

Diamond round: The trapezoid log is 8 $^3/_4$" along its longest edge. Cut 40 from the dark fabric and 40 from the light.
Stars: Make 12 selvage-to-selvage cuts 1 $^3/_4$" wide from the star fabric and cut 160 diamonds.

Inner border: Piece 2 strips 1" x 56 $^3/_4$" and 2 strips 1" x 46 $^1/_2$" from the light fabric.
Accent border: Piece 2 strips 1" x 57 $^3/_4$" and 2 strips 1" x 47 $^1/_2$" from the star fabric.
Outer border: Piece 2 strips 4 $^1/_2$" x 58 $^3/_4$" and 2 strips 4 1/2" x 55 $^1/_2$" from the dark fabric.

Pastel Cabin Stars (page 88)

Quilt size   39" x 39"
Number of blocks   16
Block size   8 $^3/_4$" finished
Log width   1 $^1/_4$" finished
Number of rounds   2 + diamond round
Border   2" finished

Fabric required
1 yard dark fabric
$^3/_4$ yard light fabric
$^2/_3$ yard star fabric
1 $^1/_4$ yards backing fabric
$^1/_2$ yard border fabric
$^1/_2$ yard binding fabric

Cutting instructions
Follow the directions for Straight Furrows. Crosscut 16 center/first light log combinations. Cut 16 sets of light logs (through 5 $^1/_2$") and 16 sets of dark logs (through 6 $^3/_4$"). The longest measurement of the trapezoid logs is 6 $^1/_4$"; cut 32 light and 32 dark. Make 9 cuts 1 $^3/_4$" wide from star fabric and cut 128 diamonds.

Border: Cut 2 strips 2 $^1/_2$" x 35 $^1/_2$" and 2 strips 2 $^1/_2$" 39 $^1/_2$".

Red Hot Stars (back cover; diagram on page 120)

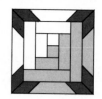

I added a narrow black border because the quilt was photographed as an unquilted top; you might want to omit the border and simply bind the quilt in a dark fabric.

Quilt size	55" x 64"	**Fabric required**
Number of blocks	42	2 ¹/₂ yards total dark fabrics
Block size	8 ³/₄" finished	2 yards total light fabrics
Log width	1 ¹/₄" finished	1 ¹/₂ yards total star fabrics
Number of rounds	2 + diamond round	¹/₂ yard border fabric
Border	1 ¹/₄"	3 ¹/₂ yards backing fabric
		¹/₂ yard binding fabric

Cutting instructions
Follow the directions for Pastel Cabin Stars, making enough of a variety of short center/first log strip units for 42 crosscuts 1 ³/₄" wide. Cut 42 sets of light logs and 42 sets of dark logs from a variety of fabrics. Cut 84 dark trapezoid logs and 84 light trapezoid logs. Make 24 cuts 1 ³/₄" wide from a variety of star fabrics, and cut 336 diamonds.

Border: Piece 2 strips 1 ³/₄" x 53" and 2 strips 1 ³/₄" x 64 ¹/₄".

Old Glory (page 87)

This was my first Cabin Stars quilt and is still my favorite. Almost all of the fabrics are printed with either stars or stripes.

Quilt size	44" x 35"
Number of blocks	20
Block size	8 ³/₄" finished
Log width	1 ¹/₄" finished
Number of rounds	2 + diamond round

Fabric required
¹/₈-¹/₄ yard each of 7 dark fabrics
1 yard light fabric
¹/₂ yard star fabric
1 ¹/₂ yards backing fabric
¹/₂ yard binding fabric

Cutting instructions
Follow the directions for Pastel Cabin Stars, preparing centers and logs for 20 blocks. Each dark fabric is used in only one log position.

Diamond round: The diamond round is constructed so there are no partial stars around the edge of the quilt.

Cut light and dark logs for the outer rounds of blocks A, B, C, D, E, F, and G as indicated on the block diagrams. The measurements shown are always the cut measurement of the longest edge. Prepare the number of blocks listed.

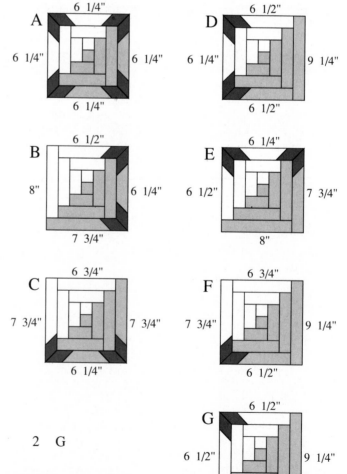

6	A	2	C	2	E	2	G
4	B	2	D	2	F		

Stars: Make 7 cuts 1 ³/₄" wide of the star fabric and cut 96 diamonds.

Stars and Stripes (page 87)

June had planned to make a modified Barn-Raising design, but modified it more than she intended by missewing the two blocks where she attached the yellow ribbons. I think the altered design looks like a shooting star.

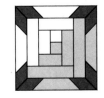

		Fabric required
Quilt size	41" x 41"	
Number of blocks	16	1 $\frac{1}{4}$ yards total dark fabrics
Block size	8 $\frac{3}{4}$" finished	$\frac{3}{4}$ yard light fabric
Log width	1 $\frac{1}{4}$" finished	1 yard star fabric (includes border)
Number of rounds	2 + diamond round	1 $\frac{1}{4}$ yards backing fabric
Border	3"	$\frac{1}{2}$ yard binding fabric

Cutting instructions

Follow the directions for Pastel Cabin Stars, using a variety of fabrics for the dark logs.

Diamond round: The diamond round is constructed so there are no partial stars around the edge of the quilt. Make 6 cuts 1 $\frac{3}{4}$" wide of the star fabric and cut 72 diamonds.

Cut light and dark logs for the outer rounds of blocks A, D, and E as indicated on the block diagrams for Old Glory, and block H as diagrammed here. The measurements shown are always the cut measurement of the longest edge. Prepare the number of blocks listed.

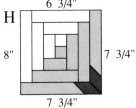

H, 6 3/4", 8", 7 3/4", 7 3/4"

- 4   A
- 4   D
- 4   E
- 4   H

Border: Cut 2 strips 3 $\frac{1}{2}$" x 35 $\frac{1}{2}$" and 2 strips 3 $\frac{1}{2}$" x 41 $\frac{1}{2}$".

Waiting for Ric (page 90)

Ginny used a contrasting fabric for the outermost logs on the "light" half of the block and a large-scale print for the "dark" half in this beautiful quilt.

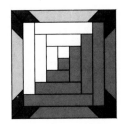

		Fabric required
Quilt size	84" x 106"	
Number of blocks	48	4 $\frac{1}{2}$ yards print fabric
Block size	11 $\frac{1}{4}$" finished	2 yards solid fabric
Log width	1 $\frac{1}{4}$" finished	1 yard contrasting fabric
Number of rounds	3 + diamond round	1 $\frac{3}{4}$ yards star fabric
Border	1 $\frac{1}{4}$" inner border,	$\frac{3}{4}$ yard inner border fabric
	7" outer border	2 yards outer border fabric
		7 yards backing fabric
		$\frac{3}{4}$ yard binding fabric

Cutting instructions

Follow the directions for Straight Furrows, using the dark measurements for the print fabric (the larger half of the block) and the light measurements for the solid fabric. Cut the trapezoids for the solid-fabric half of the block from the contrasting fabric. Prepare 48 blocks. Strip-piece the center/first log units; you will need two strip units made of print fabric and solid fabric. (If you can't make 24 crosscuts from each strip unit, you may need to piece a few additional center/first log units.) Press the seam allowances toward the solid fabric.

Diamonds: Make 28 cuts 1 $\frac{3}{4}$" wide of star fabric and cut 384 diamonds.
Inner border: Piece 2 strips 1 $\frac{3}{4}$" x 68" and 2 strips 1 $\frac{3}{4}$" x 93".
Outer border: Piece 2 strips 7 $\frac{1}{2}$" x 70 $\frac{1}{2}$" and 2 strips 7 $\frac{1}{2}$" x 107".

Dark Stars (page 89)

Three brown fabrics were used for the three rounds of this Barn-Raising design. The stars were pieced from a variety of subtle black-on-black prints.

Quilt size   67" x 67"
Number of blocks   36
Block size   11 ¼" finished
Log width   1 ¼" finished
Number of rounds   3 + diamond round

Fabric required
½ yard dark #1 (center)
1 ¾ yards dark #2
1 ¼ yards dark #3 (outer)
1 ¾ yards light fabric
1 yard total star fabrics
4 yards backing fabric
½ yard binding fabric

Cutting instructions

Follow the directions for Straight Furrows, cutting 36 sets of light logs and 4 sets of logs from dark #1, 20 from dark #2, and 12 from dark #3. Make one strip unit each for center/first log units from darks #2 and #3. Make an 8" strip unit from dark #1, or piece 4 centers and first logs.

Diamond round: The diamond round is constructed so there are no partial stars around the edge of the quilt. Make a total of 15 cuts 1 ¾" wide of the star fabrics and cut 200 diamonds.

Cut light and dark logs for the outer rounds of blocks A, B, C, D, E, and H as indicated on the block diagrams. The measurements shown are always the cut measurement of the longest edge. Prepare the number of blocks listed.

dark #1	4	A
dark #2	12	A
	4	B
	4	C
dark #3	4	D
	4	E
	4	H

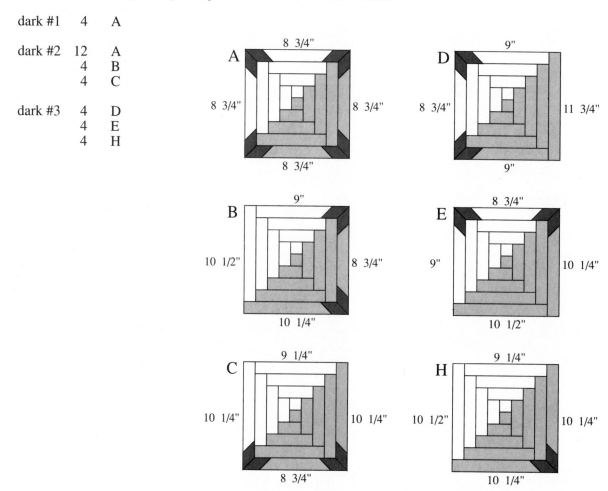

Star Wheels (page 88)

Of the 36 blocks in this quilt, 16 are made entirely of the solid background color; the other 20 blocks have the print on the large ("dark") half of the block and the solid on the small ("light") half.

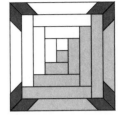

		Fabric required
Quilt size	72" x 72"	1 ³/₄ yards print pinwheel fabric
Number of blocks	36	3 ³/₄ yards solid background
Block size	11 ¹/₄" finished	fabric
Log width	1 ¹/₄" finished	1 ³/₄ yard star fabric (includes
Number of rounds	3 + diamond round	border)
Border	2 ¹/₂"	4 ¹/₂ yards backing fabric
		³/₄ yard binding fabric

Cutting instructions

Follow the directions for Straight Furrows. Cut 36 sets of the "light" logs from the solid fabric. Cut 16 sets of the "dark" logs from the solid fabric, and 20 sets from the pinwheel fabric. Speed piece the center/first log units; make one strip unit of 2 cuts of solid fabric, and another strip unit of a cut of solid fabric and a cut of pinwheel fabric. Make 20 crosscuts from the first, and 16 crosscuts from the second.

Diamond round: Make 15 cuts from the star fabric and cut 200 diamonds.
Follow the diagrams for Dark Stars and prepare the number of blocks listed. A new block, I, is diagrammed here.

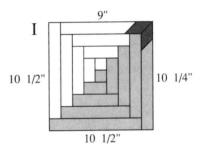

Solid blocks	8	A
	8	E
Print/solid blocks	8	A
	4	B
	4	E
	4	I

Border: Piece 2 strips 3" x 68" and 2 strips 3" x 73".

Christmas Tree #1 (page 86)

This tree is larger than Christmas Tree #2, mainly because there are three rounds before the diamond round rather than two. This also places the stars farther apart. Both trees employ two shades of background fabrics, taking advantage of the diagonal division of the log cabin block to draw a nimbus of light around the tree. The design is complex, employing eight different blocks *and* their mirror images. The piecing of the top of the quilt, in which the top star extends into the background fabric, is also a little exotic.

		Fabric required
Quilt size	50" x 70"	2 ¹/₄ yards total dark green fabrics (includes
Number of blocks	24	border)
Block size	7" x 15"	³/₄ yard total medium green fabrics
Log width	1" finished, 1" x 9" centers	1 ¹/₂ yards total white fabrics
Number of rounds	2 + diamond round	³/₄ yard total off-white fabrics
Border	1" inner border,	¹/₄ yard total brown fabrics
	3" outer border	¹/₂ yard star fabric
		3 ¹/₂ yards backing fabric
		¹/₂ yard binding fabric

Cutting instructions

Dark green, brown, and off-white are used only for the large ("dark") half of the blocks. Medium green and white are used for only the small ("light") half of the blocks. The only exceptions are the two trunk blocks G, in which off-white is used for the light logs.

Light logs: Cut 6 sets from medium green fabrics, 16 sets from white fabrics, and 2 sets from off-white fabrics.

    1 1/2" x 5" (center)
    1 1/2" x 9 1/2"
    1 1/2" x 2 1/2"
    1 1/2" x 11 1/2"
    1 1/2" x 4 1/2"

Dark logs: Cut 12 sets from dark green fabrics, 10 sets from off-white fabrics, and 2 sets from brown fabrics.

    1 1/2" x 5" (center)
    1 1/2" x 10 1/2"
    1 1/2" x 3 1/2"
    1 1/2" x 12 1/2"
    1 1/2" x 5 1/2"

Inner log cabin blocks: Refer to the diagrams. The centers are made by seaming together the 5" pieces of light and dark. For each quantity listed construct half of the blocks clockwise and half counter-clockwise, making blocks that are mirror images of one another. ***The illustrations show only the clockwise blocks.***

	dark logs	light logs
6	dark green	white
6	dark green	medium green
10	off-white	white
2	brown	off-white

Diamond round: Referring to the block diagrams, cut the logs for the diamond rounds. If you are making the quilt scrappy, refer to the inner blocks you just pieced when selecting fabrics for the outer rounds. Cut and piece the quantity listed below. Continue to construct half of the blocks clockwise and half counterclockwise.

Be careful when you cut the logs that have a diamond at only one end; half of the logs must be the mirror image of the other half. Also note that block C has one white log on the dark side, and G has one dark green log on the light side. These logs slightly round the bottom of the tree.

		dark logs	light logs
4	A	dark green	white
6	B	dark green	medium green
2	C	dark green	white
6	D	off-white	white
2	E	off-white	white
2	F	off-white	white
2	G	brown	off-white

Stars: Make 7 selvage-to-selvage cuts of star fabric each 1 1/2" wide, and cut 112 diamonds.

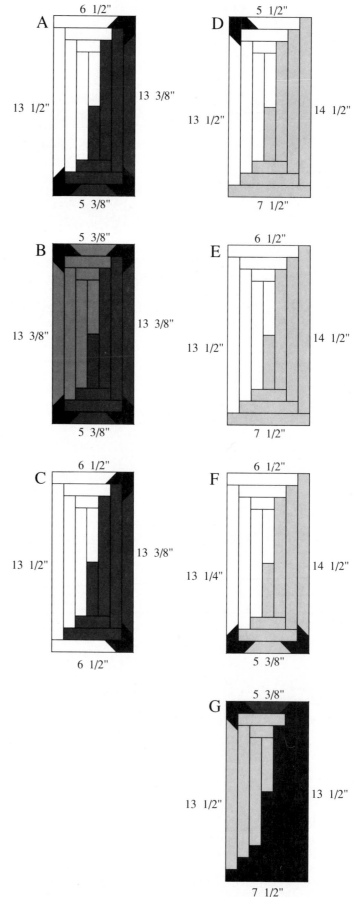

136

Assemble the blocks into the tree design, following the diagram.

TREETOP STAR AND BORDERS

Inner border: Before you finish the treetop star, add border strips to the sides and bottom of the tree. Cut pieces as listed.

    1 $\frac{1}{2}$ x 7 $\frac{1}{2}$"   4 off-white, 2 white
    1 $\frac{1}{2}$" x 15 $\frac{1}{2}$"   4 off-white, 4 white

Sew the short pieces together end-to-end for the bottom border, with off-white pieces at the ends and two in the center. Sew to the quilt. Sew the long strips together end-to-end, alternating white and off-white pieces, to make the two side borders. Sew to the quilt.

Treetop star: The top row of log cabin blocks makes only half of the treetop star. You must add two more rows of strips to the top of the quilt to complete the star.

Diamond logs: Cut 2 of each measurement from white fabrics, as mirror images.

    1 $\frac{1}{2}$" x 5 $\frac{1}{4}$"
    1 $\frac{1}{2}$" x 2 $\frac{1}{2}$"

Cut 4 pieces 1 $\frac{1}{2}$" x 8 $\frac{1}{2}$", 2 from off-white fabrics and 2 from white fabrics.
Cut 4 pieces 2 $\frac{1}{2}$" x 8 $\frac{1}{2}$", and 2 pieces 2 $\frac{1}{2}$" x 5 $\frac{1}{2}$", all from off-white fabrics.

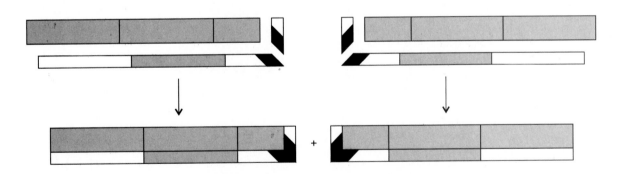

Piece as shown, as if the 2 $\frac{1}{2}$" units are the blocks to which you are attaching diamond logs: assemble the diamond logs, the sew them to two sides of each 2 $\frac{1}{2}$" unit, then miter the diamonds. Finally, sew the two halves of the top border together and sew it to the top edge of the quilt.

Outer border: Piece 2 strips 3 $\frac{1}{2}$" x 64 $\frac{1}{2}$" and 2 strips 3 $\frac{1}{2}$" x 50 $\frac{1}{2}$". Attach the sides first, then the top and bottom.

Christmas Tree #2 (page 86)

This tree is smaller than Christmas Tree #1 and the stars are closer together. Tone-on-tone fabrics are used for a cleaner, less spangly look.

Quilt size   38" x 50"
Number of blocks   24
Block size   5" x 10" finished
Log width   1" finished, 1" x 6" centers
Number of rounds   2 + diamond round

Fabric required

1 ½ yards dark green fabric (includes outer border)
¼ yard medium green fabric
1 yard total white-on-white prints (includes inner border)
½ yard total white-on-muslin prints
¼ yard brown fabric
½ yard star fabric, or scraps of several fabrics
1 ⅔ yards backing fabric
½ yard binding fabric

Cutting instructions

Dark green, brown, and off-white are used for the large ("dark") half of the blocks, and medium green and white are used for the small ("light") half. The only exceptions are the 2 G blocks, which are entirely white.

Light logs: Cut 6 sets from the medium green fabric and 18 sets from white fabrics.
  1 ½" x 3 ½" (center)
  1 ½" x 6 ½"
  1 ½" x 2 ½"

Dark Logs: Cut 12 sets from the dark green fabric, 8 sets from off-white fabrics, 2 sets from the brown fabric, and 2 sets from white fabrics.
  1 ½" x 3 ½" (center)
  1 ½" x 7 ½"
  1 ½" x 3 ½"

Inner log cabin blocks: Refer to the diagrams. The centers are made by seaming together the 3 ½" pieces of light and dark. For each quantity listed construct half of the blocks clockwise and half counterclockwise, making blocks that are mirror images of one another. ***The illustrations show only the clockwise blocks.***

	dark logs	light logs
6	dark green	white
6	dark green	medium green
8	off-white	white
2	white	white
2	brown	white

Diamond round: Referring to the block diagrams, cut the logs for the diamond rounds. Cut and piece the quantity listed below. Continue to construct half of the blocks clockwise and half counterclockwise.

Be careful when you cut the logs that have a diamond at only one end; half of the logs must be the mirror image of the other half. Also note that block D has one white log on the dark side, and H has one dark green log on the light side. These logs slightly round the bottom of the tree.

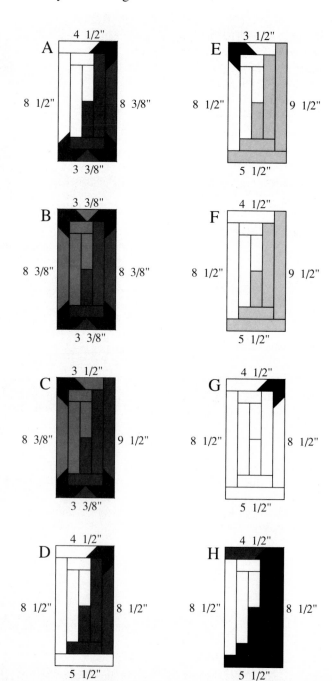

138

		dark logs	*light logs*
4	A	dark green	white
4	B	dark green	medium green
2	C	dark green	medium green
2	D	dark green	white
4	E	off-white	white
4	F	off-white	white
2	G	white	white
2	H	brown	white

Stars: If your stars will all be the same, make 6 selvage-to-selvage cuts of star fabric each 1 $\frac{1}{2}$" wide, and cut 96 diamonds. Or, if each star is to be different, cut 8 diamonds of each star fabric.

Assemble the blocks into the tree design, following the diagram.

TREETOP STAR AND BORDERS

Inner border: Before you finish the treetop star, add border strips to the sides and bottom of the tree. Cut 2 pieces 1 $\frac{1}{2}$" x 40 $\frac{1}{2}$" for the sides, and a piece 1 $\frac{1}{2}$" x 32 $\frac{1}{2}$" for the bottom.

Treetop star: Follow the directions for Christmas Tree #1. For the diamond logs, cut a mirror-image pair of each measurement from white fabrics.

> 1 $\frac{1}{2}$" x 3 $\frac{1}{4}$"
> 1 $\frac{1}{2}$" x 2 $\frac{1}{2}$"

Cut the following pieces for the narrow inner border, 2 of each measurement from off-white fabrics and 2 of each from white fabrics.

> 1 $\frac{1}{2}$" x 5 $\frac{1}{2}$"
> 1 $\frac{1}{2}$" x 7 $\frac{1}{2}$"

The 2 $\frac{1}{2}$" units are not pieced. Cut 2 pieces from a white fabric, 2 $\frac{1}{2}$" x 15 $\frac{1}{2}$".

Assemble as illustrated for Christmas Tree #1.

Outer border: Cut or piece 2 strips 3 $\frac{1}{2}$" x 44 $\frac{1}{2}$" for the sides and cut 2 strips 3 $\frac{1}{2}$" x 38 $\frac{1}{2}$" for the top and bottom.

Yellow Spools *by Lorraine Herge and Janet Kime; color plate on page 70, instructions on page 42.*

Borders

Borders on log cabin quilts are usually simple or are omitted entirely. Log cabin designs tend to be so bold and active that all you really need is a solid strip of color to corral the design.

Toys (page 61) and Scarlet Ribbons (page 85) are examples of log cabin designs that need no border; the binding alone is enough to finish the quilt. The Christmas Tree quilts (page 86) and Vashon Interweave (page 81) are more vivid and need a visually strong frame of color to contain the design. Many designs on white backgrounds, such as these, look better with a dark frame to define the edge of the quilt. As with any type of quilt, a contrasting inner border can add a lot of interest; see Watercolor (page 72) and Amish Spools (page 67).

A pieced border on a log cabin quilt should usually be constructed of squares and rectangles to echo the pieces in the log cabin blocks. One possibility is a border of stacked narrow strips. On older quilts, these borders were probably made from strips left over from piecing the blocks; nowadays, they can be quickly speed pieced. See the directions for Don and Rachel's quilt on page 63.

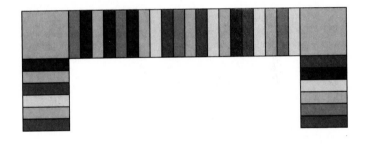

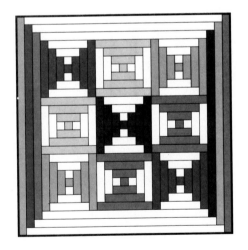

Another possibility is to treat the quilt body as if it were the center of a log cabin block, and add narrow border strips counterclockwise. Green strips were added in this manner to Pine Trees (page 75) as a subtle joke; you have to look closely at the quilt to see that it is in fact one big log cabin block. The treatment is more obvious in Old-Fashioned Courthouse Steps (page 68), in which dark strips are added to the sides and light strips to the top and bottom, echoing the block used in the quilt.

Log cabin blocks themselves make a striking border. They can be assembled into a variety of sawtooth border designs; some possibilities are illustrated on page 143. A double row of Thick-and-Thin blocks can make a pieced swag border.

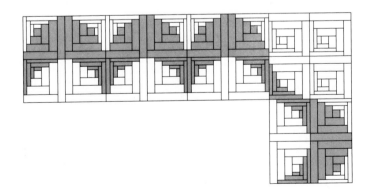

To plan a border of log cabin blocks, first determine the approximate size of the blocks. If you are adding a log cabin border to a log cabin quilt, you may want to make the border blocks a different size than those in the body of the quilt, so that the border will be distinct. Sketch at least a quarter of your quilt on graph paper, and sketch in sawtooth borders of different sizes until you arrive at one that pleases you. There is no particular rule about size; you just want something that, in your opinion, complements the main design but doesn't overwhelm it.

Once you know the approximate size of the border blocks, you need to figure out a log cabin block that will be that size. I find it easiest to work with 1" finished logs, which make blocks that are 5", 6", 7", and so on. Refer to the chapter on log cabin design for suggestions on how to change the size of your log cabin block.

It is difficult to make an intricately pieced border fit precisely around your quilt top. A very handy device is the coping strip, which is simply the inner border. You will almost always want a strip of fabric separating the body of your quilt from the border design. Use this strip to bring the quilt up to a size which will accommodate a multiple of your border blocks.

coping strip

For example, the body of the quilt Yellow Spools (page 70) was 43" x 43". I planned to use 7" border blocks. To bring the quilt sides up to 49" (7" x 7 = 49"), I added 6" to the length and width by adding a 3" inner border all around.

If your quilt is rectangular, of course, you must plan two different lengths of border strips. You may want to make the coping strip a different width on the sides than on the top and bottom, or even add a second strip to the sides only. There is no law that says that the border strips must be the same width on all four sides of the quilt.

The particular border design used for Yellow Spools would normally require an even number of log cabin blocks on each side of the quilt. Because there is an odd number of blocks, in the center of each border a Courthouse Steps block is substituted, which makes a pleasing little peak. This is a good example of a necessary adjustment that actually improves the design. It is these little surprises that make pieced borders so much fun.

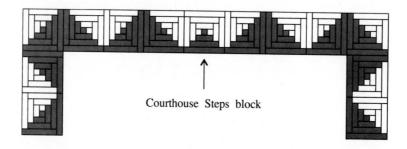

Courthouse Steps block

Sample log cabin border designs (6x6) Each border is six blocks wide. With the four corner blocks, the total number of log cabin blocks needed is 28.

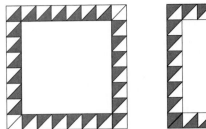 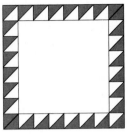  

Sample log cabin border designs (8x8) Each border is eight blocks wide. With the four corner blocks, the total number of log cabin blocks needed is 36.

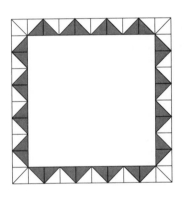 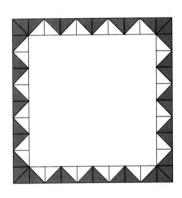 

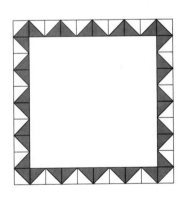  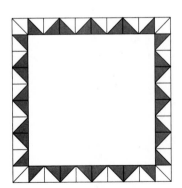

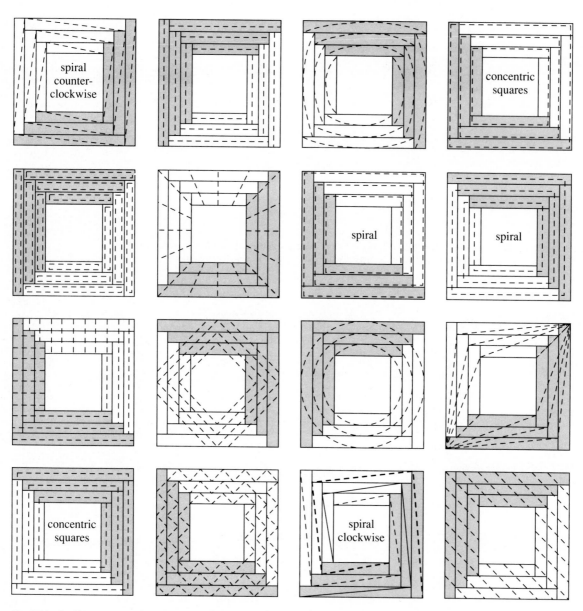

Each block of the quilt Toys (page 61) was hand quilted in a different design.

Quilting Designs

Log cabin quilts can be hand quilted, machine quilted, or tied. (Or if you have had all you can take with a particular quilt top, you can hem it and use it as a tablecloth.) Because there are so many seam allowances to cross, many log cabin quilts are machine quilted. However, there are a variety of ways to hand quilt the blocks that avoid most or all of the seam allowances.

I prepared Toys (page 61) as a quilting sampler, quilting each of the 16 blocks in a different design. After the first eight or ten designs my ideas were a little impractical, but none was difficult to quilt. The Toys designs are shown on the facing page.

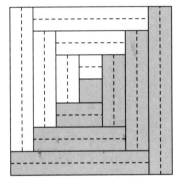

One of the easiest ways to hand quilt log cabin blocks is to quilt down the center of each log. This method avoids all of the same allowances, if you pressed all seam allowances toward the outside of the block as suggested in the directions. Also, because the quilting lines divide each log in half lengthwise, the blocks will look as though they are composed of twice as many narrow logs.

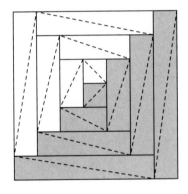

One of my favorite variations of quilting down the center of each log is quilting from corner to corner down the length of the log. I like the off-kilter look this provides; it can add a lot of movement to an otherwise tame quilt. If you start at the inside corner of the smallest log and quilt in the same direction in which the log was pieced (clockwise or counterclockwise), you can stitch a continuous line from the center to the outer edge, with no jumps or breaks.

If you quilt in the direction opposite to that in which the block was pieced, you will have to start and stop three concentric spirals; rather a lot of bother for a similar visual effect.

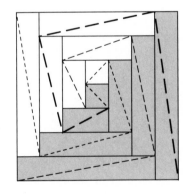

Another modification of quilting down the center of each log is to quilt a long curve down each log. You avoid almost all the seam allowances, and this method adds some curves to your very angular pieced design. I used this method in the Spring Flowers and Cabin Rose quilts (pages 74 and 76) to soften the angular flowers and imitate the curved edges of petals and leaves.

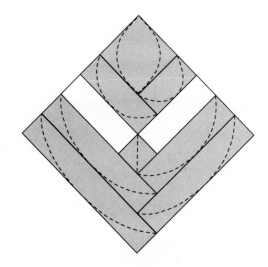

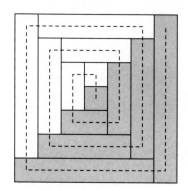

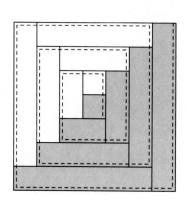

You can quilt each block in a continuous line, starting at the center and spiraling from the inside to the outside. You can do this down the center of the logs, or "in the ditch," just inside the seamline. The seam allowances, if you pressed them to the outside of the block, are on the outside side of the seamline, so quilt on the other side.

You can also quilt the blocks in concentric squares, either down the centers of the logs or in the ditch.

I often quilt in the ditch because it highlights each individual log. Sometimes quilting down the center of each log interferes with my enjoyment of the printed designs on the fabric; quilting in the ditch allows the viewer to see all there is of each piece of fabric.

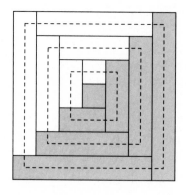

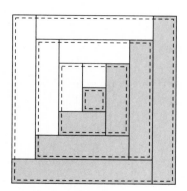

*Detail, **Spring Flowers**. From the back of the quilt you can see the curved quilting lines. The graceful border was drawn freehand.*

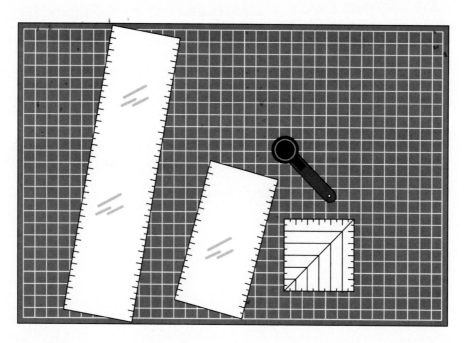

The minimum amount of equipment you will need for rotary cutting is a cutter, a special mat, and a 24" acrylic ruler. A 6x12" ruler and a 6" square ruler with the 45° angle marked are also useful.

Quiltmaking Techniques

General Sewing Techniques

Seams All seams are $1/4$" wide. It is very important that your seam width be exact. Mark a $1/4$" seam width on the throat plate of your sewing machine with a piece of masking tape, and line up the raw edges of your fabric with the masking tape as you sew. Sew with a medium-length straight stitch, 10-12 stitches per inch. Sew seams from raw edge to raw edge. It is not necessary to backstitch any seam that will be crossed by a subsequent seam, which is almost always the case in log cabin blocks. You may want to backstitch on the outer round to prevent the seams from pulling apart at the edges as the block is handled.

It is often difficult to decide what color of thread to use when sewing log cabin blocks, because light logs are sewn to dark logs. I generally use either thread that matches the lighter color (so any loose ends will not show through the quilt top as dark threads might) or neutral grey or medium brown thread.

Pressing When machine sewing, always press a seam before crossing it with another seam. Do not press seam allowances open; instead, press all seam allowances to one side. Press from the back, and then press again from the front, flattening out the bump of the seam.

Rotary cutting

Tools In addition to a rotary cutter, you will need a special rotary-cutting mat and at least one acrylic ruler, $1/8$" thick and 24" long. A 6" square acrylic ruler comes in very handy and is indispensible if you plan to make a Cabin Stars quilt. A 12" acrylic ruler is convenient for cutting smaller pieces.

CAUTION: Be very careful with the rotary cutter; the blade is very sharp. Never leave it where children can find it. The mat will last a long time if you are careful not to expose it to heat. Don't leave it in your car on a sunny day, and don't set your coffee mug down on it.

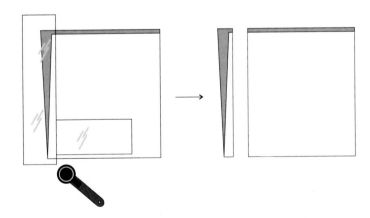

Clean-up cut To prepare your fabric for rotary cutting, machine wash and machine dry it, then refold it the way it was on the bolt, selvages together. Lay the fabric on the cutting mat with the fold toward you and the selvages away from you. Match the selvages rather than the raw edges; the fabric should lie flat along the fold and not ripple.

Line up the edge of your small acrylic ruler with the fold, then line up the long ruler against the small ruler. Remove the small ruler and cut the fabric. You now have a crisp edge that is exactly perpendicular to the fold. This is called "cleaning up the edge."

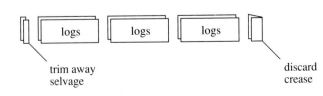

trim away selvage

discard crease

You are now ready to cut your logs. Move the ruler in from the left (from the right if you are left-handed), measuring and cutting strips. These strips are often referred to as cuts, or selvage-to-selvage cuts. Trim off the selvages (*always*) and cut your logs the lengths needed, cutting from the trimmed edges toward the fold. Try to arrange your cuts so you can throw away a little piece with the fold in it; the crease mark is difficult to remove.

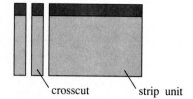

crosscut   strip unit

Strip units Rotary-cut strips are often sewn together lengthwise to make *strip units*. After pressing your strip unit thoroughly, measure in from the left edge with your ruler and cut off sections; these are called *crosscuts*. If when constructing a strip unit made of several strips you have trouble with a curve developing, try sewing pairs of strips together top to bottom, then sewing the pairs to each other bottom to top.

Setting the Quilt

After you have assembled all of your blocks, you must sew them together into the quilt top. This is called *setting the quilt*.

Most log cabin quilts are very easy to set. Sew the blocks together into rows (with ¼" seams, again). Press these seam allowances all in one direction in the first row, in the opposite direction in the second row, and so on. Then sew the rows together into the quilt top.

Strips of fabric between the blocks are called *sashing strips*. Log cabin quilts are usually not sashed, as the strips would interfere with the overall design. If your design calls for sashing strips, cut short strips and sew them between the blocks as you assemble the rows. Then sew the rows together with long sashing strips in

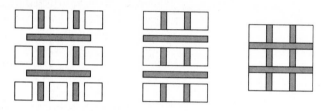

between. Press all seam allowances toward the sashing strips. Some quilts have small squares or little pieced blocks where the sashing strips intersect. These are called *set blocks*.

The set illustrated above is a *straight set*. In some of the quilts in this book the blocks are turned sideways, which is called *on point*. Again, the blocks are sewn into rows, with or without sashing strips, and then the rows are sewn together. However, you must add triangles to the end of each row and at the corners to square up the quilt. The measurements for the triangles are provided in the instructions for each quilt in this book.

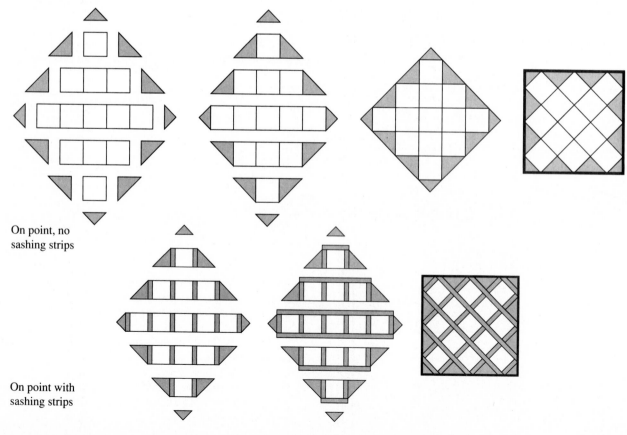

On point, no
sashing strips

On point with
sashing strips

Borders

After the blocks have been set, you may add a border to your quilt. The simplest border is a wide strip of fabric sewn to each side of the quilt. To add a simple squared border, sew border strips to the two sides and press, then add the top and bottom borders and press. Unless otherwise stated, the border measurements in this book are for simple squared borders.

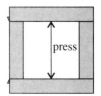

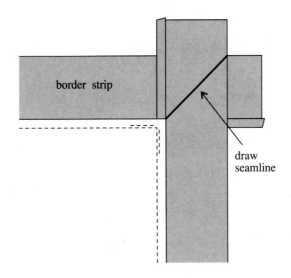

border strip

draw seamline

If you prefer to miter the corners of your border, cut each border strip the length of that side of the quilt, plus three times the width of the border. This allows the amount you need at each end for the miter, plus a little extra for safety.

Sew all four border strips on before you make the miters. Use 1/4" seams, and start and stop 1/4" in from the corners. Backstitch for strength. Do not press the seam allowances yet.

To mark the miter, lay a corner of the quilt out flat, wrong side up. Straighten out the long ends of the border strips so they are exactly lined up with the edges of the quilt, crossing at right angles. On the wrong side of the border strip on top, draw the miter seamline as shown.

Switch the strips so the other one is on top and draw the other miter seamline on its wrong side. Pin the miter seam, right sides together, matching the seamlines. Sew the miter, starting at the inside corner and backstitching, and sewing out to the point. Trim away all but a 1/4" seam allowance and press the seam open. Repeat on the other three corners.

The Quilt Back

After the quilt top is completed, you must prepare the quilt back. Then you must baste together the back, batting, and top to prepare the quilt for machine or hand quilting.

The quilt back Prepare a quilt back that is about 2" larger all around than your quilt top. If your quilt is more than 42" wide, you will need to piece the back or purchase special fabric that is 60" or 90" wide.

For a large back 80" or so wide, simply piece two lengths of fabric together with a long center seam.

For a smaller back 40"-80" wide, add a strip along one side, or (if you prefer the symmetrical approach) sew narrower strips to both sides.

If you are making a scrappy quilt, you can have a lot of fun with your quilt back by piecing together several odds and ends, or even adding left-over blocks. If your quilt top is more formal, you will probably want a more formal and symmetrical back.

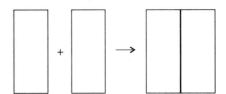

Basting the quilt

Purchase packaged batting intended for the type of finishing you plan: hand quilted, machine quilted, or tied.

To baste your quilt together, tape the back out on the floor (wrong side up!) and lay the batting on top. Smooth the quilt top over the batting and pin through all the layers here and there around the edge. Now crawl around on the quilt and hand baste the layers together with 1" stitches, in horizontal and vertical lines about 3" apart. *Always baste with white thread.* Also baste all around the quilt about 1/4" in from the edge; this will hold the edges together when you add the binding later.

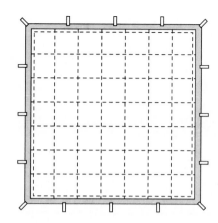

Quilting

Hand quilting Put the basted quilt in a hoop or quilting frame. Start in the center of the quilt and quilt in sections toward the edges, moving the hoop as necessary. Use short quilting needles called *betweens*, and the heavier thread sold as hand-quilting thread. You will also need a quilting thimble, which is like a regular thimble except that it is indented on the end rather than rounded out.

Tie a small knot in the end of the thread, and with the needle wiggle a hole in the surface of the quilt that you can pull the knot through, so it lodges in the batting. There should be no knots left on either the top or the bottom of the quilt.

Use a running stitch for hand quilting. Push the needle through the fabric with a quilting thimble on your third finger. Keep your other hand under the quilt and follow the progress of the needle with your second or third finger. This finger will get sore, as it gets poked a lot, but you will build up a callus. There are several special thimbles on the market for this under-the-quilt finger, and you may want to try them. Most quilters just suffer.

1. Start the needle through the quilt almost vertically.
2. Push up on the fabric from under the quilt, as you rock the needle back until it is almost horizontal.
3. Push the needle through the bump you have made.
4. Rock the needle back to vertical and repeat. When you have three or four stitches on the needle, pull it through.

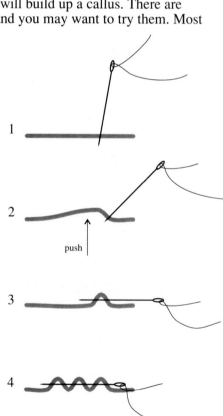

As you push up from underneath and rock the needle back, you are keeping the fabric and needle almost perpendicular. This rocking motion as you push the needle through with the end of the thimble allows you to take small stitches in spite of the thickness of the quilt. As is true of many things in life, your quilting will improve with practice. At first, concentrate on keeping your stitches about the same length and in a straight line. As you become more skilled, your stitches will become smaller.

When you reach the end of your thread or a stopping place in your design, take a few stitches back and forth through the batting and cut the thread even with the surface of the quilt.

Machine quilting If you chose to machine quilt your project, baste it well first. Some quilters fasten the layers together with safety pins about 4" apart, partly because it is faster and partly because long basting stitches tend to get caught on the machine presser foot.

You can quilt just about any design by machine, but for your first project stick to straight lines. If you start and end the lines out at the edges of the quilt, the beginnings and ends of the stitching lines will be covered by the binding. Otherwise, backstitch at the beginning and end of each line of machine quilting.